d.
HASSO PLATTNER
Institute of Design at Stanford

# make space

**How to Set the Stage for Creative Collaboration**

Scott Doorley & Scott Witthoft

with a foreword by David Kelley

Space matters. We read our
physical environment
like we read a human face.

Half-Title Page

# make space

**WILEY**

John Wiley & Sons, Inc.
This book is printed on acid-free paper.

Here's how you can get permission to reproduce this material.

Library of Congress
Cataloging-in-Publication Data

Doorley, Scott.; Witthoft, Scott.
Make space : How to Set the Stage for Creative
Collaboration / Scott Doorley & Scott Witthoft ;
foreword by David Kelley.
   p. cm.
 Includes index.
ISBN 978-1-118-14372-8 (cloth : alk. paper);
ISBN 978-1-118-17251-3 (ebk); ISBN 978-1-
118-17252-0 (ebk); ISBN 978-1-118-17253-7
(ebk); ISBN 978-1-118-19731-8 (ebk); ISBN
978-1-118-19732-5 (ebk)
1. Architectural design. 2. Architecture-
-Psychological aspects. 3. Work
environment--Psychological aspects. I. Witthoft,
Scott. II. Title. III. Title: How to set the stage for
creative collaboration.
NA2750.D665 2012
729--dc23
2011031421

Printed in the United States of America

10 9 8 7 6 5 4 3 2 1

One of these numbers is removed with each edition printed. So if there's still a "1," this is a first edition. What happens if there's an 11th edition? We don't know.

# Foreword_by David Kelley

Consciously or not, we feel and internalize what the space tells us about how to work. When you walk into most offices, the space tells you that it's meant for a group of people to work alone. Closed-off desks sprout off of lonely hallways, and in a few obligatory conference rooms a huge table ensures that people are safely separated from one another. Most work spaces were designed according to an industrial labor model, from a time when our work was tethered to big machines and our status was rooted in the size of our office space.

When I started IDEO with friends in 1978, I knew we had to work differently. We were engineers and still wore ties, but we sat in a circle on the floor for meetings. It made everyone feel equal and allowed us a certain kind of openness with each other. Since then, at IDEO and the d.school, space has been a foundation for the expression of our cultural values. We value innovation as a team sport; it needs "we" spaces more than conventional "I" spaces.

Collaboration and creation aren't bound to designated areas; they evolve throughout a space, absorbing different people, places, and perspectives.

Space and its impact on behavior have been important to me from those earliest days, through IDEO and my long association with Steelcase. At the d.school, it's been a critical element in creating a different kind of educational environment, one that nourishes creative confidence in our students. One of our first challenges was to equalize the respective status of students and faculty. When you walk into one of our classes, it's almost impossible to tell who's teaching and who's learning. Innovation thrives on this kind of equality. With a boss or a professor standing at the head of the room, it feels like a "sage on stage"—people are reluctant to share their ideas ("What if the boss doesn't like it?"). Reconfiguring the physical relationship is a powerful signal that participation is truly welcome. The result is that you get better ideas out in the open, where they can grow. But

there's not just one ideal design for a collaborative space. The people using it should be able to transform it themselves, move things around, and create what they need for the work they're doing at the moment.

Our students have responded to this in ways that have surpassed our biggest hopes. They come from very different backgrounds and very different places on campus and experience their deepest collaborations here. When our alumni—from school administrators to entrepreneurs—start their own organizations, they build their spaces around these same values.

Regardless of whether it's a classroom or the offices of a billion-dollar company, space is something to think of as an instrument for innovation and collaboration. It's not an initial, given condition, something that should be accepted as is. Space is a valuable tool that can help you create deep and meaningful collaborations in your work and life.

When we started the d.school, we were stuck with a double-wide trailer no one else wanted, the team leading our space design efforts had little prior expertise in the field, and we were told we would have to move every 12 months for years before our first official space would be available.

These apparently unfortunate initial conditions are not obvious when you walk into our newly renovated building at the heart of the Stanford campus. In hindsight, the path we were forced to take appears close to inspired.

The yearly moves turned out to be a profound forcing function for learning, not just about space, but for prototyping and evolving our entire organization. And having a team lead the way that seemingly had no business designing spaces set the stage for unexpected approaches to emerge. We weren't looking for a groovy office. We were looking to create learning experiences for our students, make it safe for them to fail, and provoke an ecosystem as complex as Stanford to change. The members of our team had experience that was perfectly suited to this challenge.

We have had the opportunity to be a bit more radical than others might feel is safe in their workplace. And we have been able to test our rapidly evolving ideas with real people every day—with the thousands of students who have come to the d.school to learn how to be better innovators, and with their teachers and project partners, too.

At first, we used space to support the activities of our teams, as a signal that the d.school was a different kind of place, and as a way to embody our values. We put team spaces and couches in classrooms to facilitate project work and allow for moments of debriefing. We removed carpet to expose concrete floors to make it clear that the d.school is a work space, not an office space. And we put desks near the entrance so that people are the first thing you see when you walk in, reinforcing that one of our principal values is human-centeredness.

Along the way, we learned that we have to prototype our way into any new space; to continuously iterate, adapt, and evolve our spaces after we move in; and to think of space primarily as a way to change behavior, not as a facilities project or a showpiece for our brand. We want our teams to act in more empathetic ways, so we make our spaces more human, with more places to debrief, reflect, and connect. We want our teams to work collaboratively instead of individually, so we have generous collaboration spaces and "bare essential" individual spaces. We want our teams to get up and try stuff, not sit around and talk in long meetings, so we make seating uncomfortable and the tables too small. Supplies, tools, and workbenches are more apparently available than conference phones and conference tables. We want leadership to move around to the person who has the relevant expertise at the time, not just to the person in charge, so we create huddle rooms without explicit status associated. There's no head of the table or front of the classroom.

We want our students and teams to be mindful of space and to take responsibility for setting up the environments that will amplify their work. So we set the expectation that each person is a steward of the space, that they need to care for it. At the same time, if it's not working, they change it or, better yet, hack it.

This book is an attempt to capture what the d.school adventure has taught us along the way and is a tool to help you to use space to develop your unique culture. I hope our story is an encouragement to you, suggesting that big things often have small beginnings, that radical change usually starts with brave but little steps, and that when people feel safe to try something new, spectacular things can happen. Good luck as you make space in your life, your teams, and your organization to innovate!

# instructions

## tools

**Make the useful things that fill up a space—furniture, storage options, materials, etc.**

make space is a tool for using space to shape the culture and habits of a creative community. Building a space is tough, but shaping culture is an absurd act of daring. It's like assembling a 10,000 piece puzzle. On a grass field. During a hurricane. And the puzzle itself is a photo of a grass field. At 1:1 scale. Address this conundrum with action. Begin to deliberately alter your environment and you will reveal what enhances collaboration and what doesn't, what boosts creativity and what doesn't. Reconfiguring, prototyping, and building are the equivalent of starting a puzzle with the corners: a simple approach that illuminates a structure to attach more complex issues. The most difficult part of any of these actions is simply getting started, this book is filled with ways to start transforming your space. Many can be accomplished in hours, some in minutes.

make space has five different types of content: Tools, Situations, Design Template, Space Studies, and Insights. Individual entries from each are shuffled throughout the book and are described in more detail over there. We designed this book so that you would put it down—so that you can and will experiment.

Read it long enough to get inspired, then put it aside and get to work. Pick it up when you need another boost, then put it down again and get back to work.

Each entry and the sum of their collisions can help you quickly fine-tune every decision you make—from the shape & scale of the furniture you use to the music you play in the space—to inspire new ways of working and interacting.

Tools range from DIY "hacks" that may take a matter of hours, to examples of CNC milled furniture you'll likely need assistance in building. If you are a maker at heart or just can't wait to try out some stuff, these will get you going. The rolling whiteboard Z-Rack (page 16) is a popular project that is not too difficult to construct. Each Tool spread features build instructions, tips, and sourcing information.

# 9

# situations

**Quick, repeatable configurations or patterns, usually at the scale of a room.**

Some Situations take as little effort as simply rearranging existing furniture in a few minutes or even seconds; others require some consideration and construction. For example, "Around the Campfire" (page 32) is an easy pattern that has instant impact. The Situations featured here offer a starting point for shaping your space—create your own variations for best effect.

# design template

**A comprehensive breakdown of the elements at play in a space, or the game behind the game.**

This book is about space only insomuch as it affects people. The design template deciphers how the sense of a place and the properties of the things within it spark creative and collaborative attitudes and actions. The template is based on the "Attitudes" in our particular culture (page 51) that may match or oppose those in yours. In any case it is still a great place to start the groundwork for intentionally playing with space.

# space studies

**First-person dispatches from the front lines of space design.**

Interspersed throughout **make space** are real-life case studies and candid essays from practicing designers, teachers, artists, entrepreneurs, managers, and researchers who have put a number of these concepts to good use. Read these to understand how people are tackling issues similar to those you face. They offer a wealth of insights within their narratives. Check out how ITP, New York University's cutting-edge digital media program, encourages students to evolve the space to suit their needs with giant "erector sets" (page 226).

# insights

**Kernels of understanding we've discovered through our "trials and errors."**

Some are hunches that seem to hold true, others are well-known tenets that we've successfully put to use. There is no substitute for doing it yourself, but we hope you'll be able to take advantage of these Insights with a little less of the heavy lifting we endured in discovering them. We've found playing with the principles in the "Design for Primates" Insight (page 23) to be very fruitful.

# Making Space for Change

## by Scott Doorley and Scott Witthoft

# Space Studies_Making Space for Change

The d.school is everywhere at Stanford. Our students come from all disciplines and take what they've learned back to their respective departments and the map of our past locations on campus is almost as far-reaching as our current impact. Since the founding of our first physical teaching space, the entire d.school has moved four times in as many years. That's a lot of moving, even for a dynamic organization focused on building adaptable innovators.

With each move, we were forced to occupy and modify spaces we would not have instinctively chosen. In responding to the scale and character of each building, we've recognized that a tool for designing creative spaces is to create smart parameters that themselves stimulate mindful modification. So began our love of improvisation.

**Birch Modular:
Be Not Precious**
Double-wide trailer on the outskirts of campus

Birch—a twenty-year-old "temporary" trailer—was such a mess that the d.school's executive director, George Kembel, feared we'd have to return our funding if our principal donor saw the place. But Birch's obscure location and shabby condition signaled permission to experiment. And that's exactly what we did. Carpets were torn out, walls were repeatedly demolished and rebuilt, and we drilled into everything—including the floors—with abandon. Birch is where we found our tone: experiment wildly and consider nothing precious.

top: Birch Modular during demolition & construction.

bottom: Birch in action with spaces for staff & students.

### Sweet Hall, 2nd Floor: Change Everything
On-campus office building

Sweet Hall was filled with offices, so we tore everything out of the entire second floor. With nothing left but the concrete floor, we turned the whole space into a roller rink of sorts by putting everything on wheels. With couches, tables, and walls completely mobile, we reconfigured everything at least every few weeks, sometimes daily. These rolling assets allowed us to do incredible things like prototype a full-scale design building for elementary school kids on a Thursday and run a group of Fortune 500 executives through a workshop that same weekend. The fun of this flexibility taught us limits, though, as even our closest collaborators felt disoriented when landmarks like the copy machine migrated overnight.

### Building 524: Experiment with Special Spaces
100-year-old loft building
in the center of campus

Sweet Hall was a fluid work space. Building 524 was literally a fluid dynamics laboratory, filled with flumes and water tanks, and a very particular dank smell. We experimented at 524 with making distinct micro-environments by overhauling ten former PhD offices into collaboration concepts—ranging from plush lounges to an all-whiteboard room. In having these options, teams could tune their activities by choosing a particular space.

Sweet Hall during class. Teams sit together in-the-round before switching into an activity.

Building 524 before the flood, but after the fluids lab. The building prior to d.school modification.

## Building 550:
## Preserve the Spirit of the Move
Our second 100-year-old loft building
in central campus

The end of our itinerant arc, Building
550 was the original drafting studio for
the campus. On sunny days, as the tall,
lofted ceilings fill with natural light, this
lovely environment once again serves as
a perfect platform for what is next.
But where to next? The product of all
these moves has been the move cycle itself, forcing constant transitions among
the different modes of Build, Reflect,
and Refresh. We always knew we'd
be moving, so we never invested too
much, and an experimental attitude
gave us permission to purge things that
weren't working.
    Currently, we're focusing on
staying in motion while remaining in
place. This includes actively preserving
the posture of prototyping by keeping
quarterly updates, maintaining spaces
like the Concept Car (page 74) for
front-and-center experimentation, and
encouraging the ebb and flow of boundaries in the midst of our work, learning,
and social spaces. We appreciate our
current environment as an embodiment
of our journey and as an agent for directions we may take in the future.

The d.school was founded in July 2003 by
David Kelley and George Kembel along with a
small group of Stanford faculty and Bay Area
design practitioners with the financial support
of Hasso Plattner. It moved into its first
home in 2005 and now resides in Building 550
at Stanford University.

Scott Doorley is Creative Director and Co-
Director of the Environments Collaborative at
the Stanford University d.school. He was a
d.school Fellow from 2006 to 2007.

Scott Witthoft is Co-Director of the
Environments Collaborative at the Stanford
University d.school. He was a d.school Fellow
from 2008 to 2009.

top: Trusses above
the Bay Studio in
Building 550.

bottom: Class
in session within
a studio.

# Easy-to-build dry-erase surfaces transform the working style of a space.

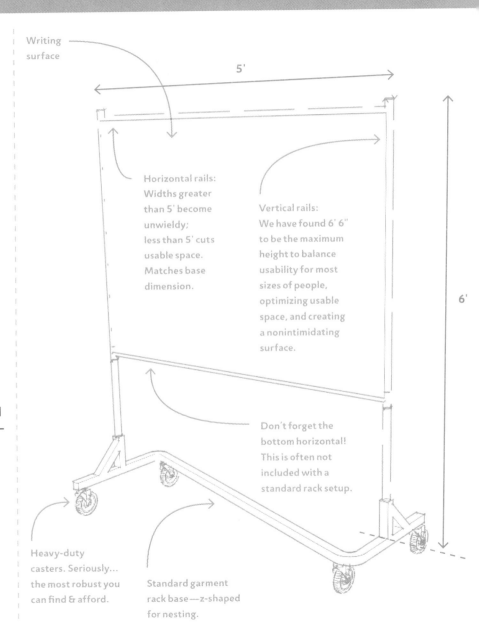

Writing surface

5'

Horizontal rails: Widths greater than 5' become unwieldy; less than 5' cuts usable space. Matches base dimension.

Vertical rails: We have found 6' 6" to be the maximum height to balance usability for most sizes of people, optimizing usable space, and creating a nonintimidating surface.

6'

Don't forget the bottom horizontal! This is often not included with a standard rack setup.

Heavy-duty casters. Seriously... the most robust you can find & afford.

Standard garment rack base—z-shaped for nesting.

# z-rack

One of the most enduring artifacts in the d.school, the Z-Rack, is actually a modified garment rack. When outfitted with a common construction material— showerboard—the Z-Rack becomes a deployable dry-erase surface.

This model is a fraction of the cost of a typical rolling dry-erase board, super-sturdy, easy to build, and large enough to act as a partition in the work space. The Z-Rack is great for subdividing large areas and creating differently scaled team work spaces.

## build instructions

### writing surface construction

Create a sandwich of showerboard panels laminated to a center panel of $1/2$" -thick foamboard or $1/4$" plywood. The result will be a dual-sided, rigid surface. It can be tricky to balance overall panel stiffness with weight—the center panel should be as stiff & light as possible.

### writing surface attachment

Attach the writing surface to the Z-Rack frame using perforated galvanized steel strapping. Drill through-holes in the writing surface and attach at the two top & two bottom corners along the horizontal rails.

Metal strap attachment

### showerboard or tileboard

The surface of this standard construction material works very well as an inexpensive and hackable alternative to commercially produced dry-erase surfaces. Eventually the surface will start to show residue and "ghosting"; water and a towel work surprisingly well for cleaning!

## sourcing

### garment ("Z") racks

The d.school has used the 6' tall double-rail Z-Racks with 4'- and 5'-long bases; locking casters are available at additional cost. Sean James Enterprises, Inc. (425 Tribble Gap Road, Cumming, GA 30040; 888 866-9826; www.garmentrack.com)

### showerboard

Showerboard is available at most home centers and local lumber suppliers. Pine Cone Lumber (895 East Evelyn Avenue, Sunnyvale, CA 94086; 408 736-5491; www.pineconelumber.com)

### foamboard

Arch Supplies (99 Missouri, San Francisco, CA 94107; 415 433-2724; www.archsupplies.com) ULINE Shipping Supply Specialists (800 958-5463; www.uline.com)

### casters

Industrial Caster & Wheel Co. (2200 Carden Street, San Leandro, CA 94577; 510 569-8303; www.icwco.com). Reference Stanford d.school red caster in 3" or 5". California Caster and Hand Truck Company (1400 17th Street, San Francisco, CA 94107; 800 950-8750; www.californiacaster.com)

### hardware

Perforated steel strapping and flexible steel "tape" are available at local hardware stores and home centers. McMaster-Carr (600 North County Line Road, Elmhurst, IL 60126; 630 600-3600; www.mcmaster.com)

## see also

**26**
Tools_HACK: Showerboard Dry-Erase Surface

**58**
Tools_Whiteboard Sliders

**190**
Tools_Writable Surfaces Everywhere

# foam cubes

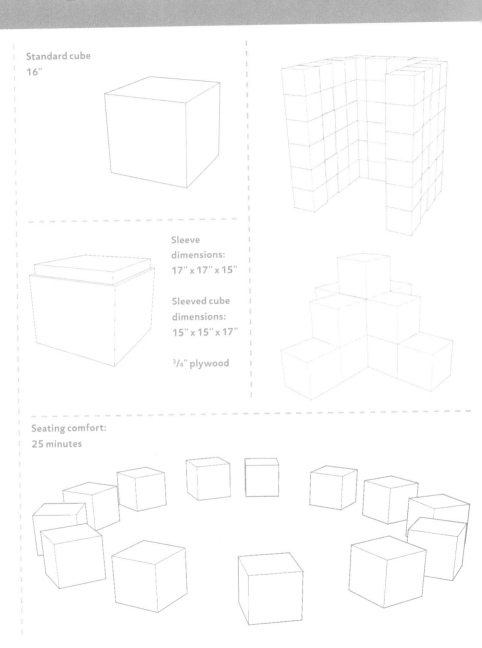

Standard cube
16"

Sleeve
dimensions:
17" x 17" x 15"

Sleeved cube
dimensions:
15" x 15" x 17"

3/4" plywood

Seating comfort:
25 minutes

Foam cubes are solid & light, and compact & stackable. They represent an abstract shape, easily adapted to imaginative uses. They can be used equally well for low seating during short conversations as for simulating elements of 3-D space at scale.*

What would it be like to make a wall here? Build it! We've seen the cubes configured into beds, a dark, enclosed room to simulate a "blind man's house," and a cube "castle," setting the stage for brainstorming on the topic of security.

The cubes are plain, which seems to be a key to their successful implementation. Their lack of ornamentation has been critically important to their use as abstract "building blocks." We've tried many different colors and shapes of cubes, and the best choice always seems to be gray.

Cubes are comfortable seats for about 25 minutes, so keep this in mind!

We've built another option, the Sleeved Cube, that adds a new dimension and makes a more comfortable seat. The plywood sleeve on this cube confines the foam and makes it comfortable for a longer period. Sleeved Cubes can also be flipped on their sides to create firm seating and different stacking surfaces.

The d.school uses approximately 150 cubes for a 50-student class; 20 cubes is a good starting quantity.

## what to buy

We've looked at two criteria in sourcing foam—the density and the indentation force deflection (IFD). The gut-feeling translation of these criteria from someone picking up or sitting on a cube might be weight and stiffness. A good range for density is from 2.0 to 4.0; less than 2.0 might feel too light; greater than 4.0 might feel too heavy. A good range for IFD is 70 to 90; less than 70 is often too squishy or soft; greater than 90 is too stiff or rigid. The density of the cubes we have used most recently is 2.0 and their IFD is 70.

## sourcing

Bob's Foam Factory (4055 Pestana Place, Fremont, CA 94538; 510 657-2420; www.bobsfoam.com)
Foamorder (1325 Howard Street, San Francisco, CA 94103 ; 415 503-1188; www.foamorder.com)
Foam 'n More (1925 West Maple Road, Troy, MI 48084; www.foamforyou.com)

*Special thanks to the IDEO Boston office for lending us our first set of cubes.

## start

Have some milk crates or sturdy cardboard boxes lying around? Set up a prominent stack for general use and see what happens. Use some of them as informal seating for your next meeting. (Note: If you use boxes, they might need internal supports to function as sturdy seats.)

## see also

**32**
Situations_Around the Campfire

**68**
Tools_Flip Stool

# instant /shared studio

**The Instant Studio is shared creative space that can be saturated with project work in seconds.**
Inspiration: The open-air Maekong market outside of Bangkok sits atop an active train track. Vendor tents flank the route; fruits and vegetables lie inches from the track. A train pulls through, people step to the side, and awnings contract. Once the train passes, shopping resumes immediately. This happens about eight times each day.

**Few organizations have enough space for every project team to have its own studio.**

Creative spaces resemble the Maekong market. Like the trains, projects and activities emerge and consume available space. But when a project "stalls on the tracks," the marketplace of other projects is left with inadequate space.

**Studios work because . . .**
You can spread out your work and get messy, you can immediately reengage work in progress after a pause, your tools are nearby, and evidence of your work is everywhere.

**Studios are tough because . . .**
They take up a lot of square footage that lies dormant when projects are inactive, and they can get cluttered, rendering them virtually useless.

**The Instant Studio solves this conundrum.**
It creates a space that, like the Maekong market, can be instantly engaged & expanded into an active studio. When you are finished, it can be just as quickly collapsed, leaving room for the next creative team.

**Make it easy to get started.**
You should be able to go from inkling to action nearly instantaneously—think in terms of seconds, not minutes. The longer it takes to get going, the more opportunities arise to slow things down.

**Features of an instant studio:**

**Storage Gallery**
Use open shelving, prominently placed, to provide easy access and put work in progress on display. Use bulk sheet materials or dry-erase surfaces for display.

**Whiteboard Sliders**
Use these sliding walls to create instant dividers that can also be used to capture ideas.

**Hanging options**
Pegs or other hooks on the walls provide opportunities to put work on display quickly.

**Clear defaults and resets**
Make the expectations of "creative citizenship" clear. Require participants to go through an orientation to the space. Post clear visual instructions of how to reset the space. Don't be afraid to remind folks of these reset rules.

extreme
studio

workspaces and materials
are owned by student teams

## start

Line team spaces like the Expandable
Team Spaces (page 110) along the edge
of an open space. Have project teams
collapse their work back to these home
bases when the teams are not active.
Cut foamboard Short Boards (page 200)
and drill out handles as portable work
surfaces. Install hooks to hang up the
boards in the shared space. Grab some
simple open shelving units for shared
storage as needed (available online
through McMaster-Carr).

## see also

**58**
Tools_Whiteboard Sliders

**110**
Tools_Expandable Team Spaces

**150**
Tools_Bulk Sheet Materials

**174**
Situations_Storage Gallery

**246**
Situations_Defaults

# Context Is Content.

**Space transmits culture. If there is one thing to be culled from these pages, look no further: this is it.**

We're willing to pay a premium at restaurants not just for the food but also for the experience of being in the particular environment—specifically for the way the smells, the music, the lighting, the seating, the appointments make us feel. Take advantage of this insight and translate these immersive experiences to the workplace and the classroom.

**Environments can be used not just to represent cultural values but also to inspire them.**
David Byrne, former Talking Heads front man and ever-fascinating artist, explains it this way in his 2009 TED Talk, "Creation in Reverse":

"Context largely determines what kind of music is written. Maybe the analogy applies to other forms of creation as well—painting, sculpture, programming or performance...."

"...The microphones that brought music to radios...changed the way we sang...."

"Chet Baker sang in a whisper, as did João Gilberto.... These guys were whispering in your ear, getting right get-ting right inside your head. Without microphones, this intimacy wouldn't have been heard at all. And mostly it wouldn't have been heard that well either, except in the privacy of a living room."

"It seems that creativity is adaptive, like anything else. When a space becomes available, work emerges to fill it."

**An example:**
This photo was taken on the first morning of a three-day Bootcamp in Design Thinking. We began on a train platform and asked the participants to challenge their assumptions by getting out and engaging people directly. (The project was about the morning commute.)

Passing trains made it nearly impossible to hear the short lecture we provided, but that was beside the point. The context said everything that needed to be said about getting out and engaging people.

## see also

40
Design Template_Places

43
Design Template_Properties

222
Insights_Use Objects to Create Experiences

# Design for Primates.

**We're smart apes. Deal with it. Design ways to keep our bodies moving.**

Humans are slightly evolved apes with big brains (and less hair, in most cases). The last 100 years of technological innovation in the workplace have focused on the big brain part. Books, computers, desks, offices are all focused on helping us get the most out of our brains. Okay.

**But let's look at apes and their bodies for a second.**
Visit any zoo and you'll see that apes spend time sitting—lots of it. But they also climb, crawl, swing, lie down, and wrestle. They even negotiate status in space through posture, position, and movement.

**Back to humans. Remove the desk from the equation, give people permission to assume alternative postures, and watch what happens.**
Our students are good examples: they lie on the floor, perch on the backs of couches, bounce on their toes, pace around the room, and do chin-ups on exposed beams—all during "work" sessions.

**Find ways to get the body moving, such as open space, nonprescriptive seating, and multiple seating heights.** Movement is not only healthy but it introduces opportunities for communication through body language.

As an example, when working with teams, we limit the amount of space a team has around a table so everyone must negotiate that space as a limited resource. A team of four gets a table that can be occupied fully by only two or three at a time. A bias toward tall horizontal surfaces (tables and stools) lowers the amount of energy required to move from a seated to a standing position. Once standing, it is easier to shift leadership roles and negotiate status on the fly.

## see also

18
Tools_Foam Cubes

28
Tools_Periodic Table

43
Design Template_Properties: Posture

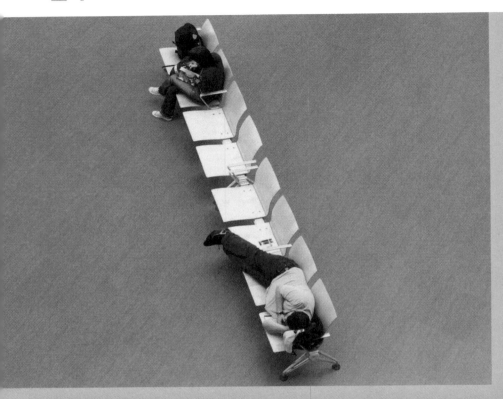

# Design with Multiple Situations in Mind.

**Almost all spaces are used in multiple ways. More often than not, the unintended use case is both more frequent and more interesting.**

A dining room doubles as a home office; a living room for adults is a playroom for kids; a kitchen becomes the primary gathering spot during a party. Design with alternate uses in mind. While you'll often find that there is more than one use for a room, it may not need to be completely and uniquely redesigned for each purpose. A room may have several general uses, but you can often group them by the kind of activities they support.

**A fun and eye-opening exercise leading to action is to reexamine a room. This is often more easily accomplished outside of your own space, but it is worth looking at locally.**
What other functions, outside of its intended use, is the room in question really being used for? Assuming you want that activity to continue, how might you quickly alter the space to support that activity?

see also

36
Insights_Follow the Hacks:
Innovation Is Everywhere

40
Design Template_Places

# A Little Prep Goes a Long Way.

**Give yourself time to prepare a space before you begin.**

Easy to say, hard to do. Schedules are often filled with back-to-back activities. But taking a moment—say, 10 or 15 minutes—to adjust a space before starting an activity can change the experience for everyone. It prompts behavior in response to a curated event rather than a haphazard gathering.

**Two simple things that can be adjusted in almost any space are orientation & ambience.**

**Orientation:** How are people positioned to engage objects or each other? Do you want the group to have shared focus on an object (say a presentation) or do you want them to be able to engage each other? If the latter, arrange chairs in a horseshoe or circle.

**Ambience:** What is the vibe or mood you are trying to create, and what is the duration of the gathering? Lowering the intensity or limiting the number of lights in a space can shift a mood from active to reflective. Opening windows (when possible) can provide some energizing fresh air for a long meeting and a little background noise that raises the energy level and increases the awareness of the surroundings.

## see also

32
Situations_Around the Campfire

44
Design Template_Properties: Orientation

45
Design Template_Properties: Ambience

246
Situations_Defaults

d.school teacher Michael Dearing prepares a "café style" environment for student teams in one of the d.school studios.

**hack**

Showerboard is the cheapest and easiest material for creating a writable wall surface.

Transform
vertical surfaces.

# showerboard
# dry-erase surface

Cut into any shape.

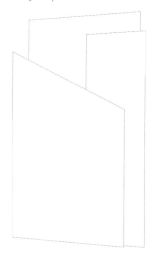

Easily mount to walls.

Showerboard or tileboard, mentioned in many Tools descriptions in this book, is a composite construction material with one nonpermeable side that works as an excellent dry-erase surface. It is intended to be hidden behind showers (what else?), but don't let that stop you from mounting it everywhere.

Unlike more expensive commercially available dry-erase surfaces, showerboard can be cut using a hand- or table saw. It can be drilled easily and mounts to walls with standard screws.

Cheap sheets! Showerboard also comes in 4' x 8' sheets, often for less than $20 a sheet—that's more than an order of magnitude cheaper than the equivalent commercial product. However, unlike diamonds, shower board is not forever and it will eventually lose its sheen. For what it does and what it costs, though, it'll serve its unexpected purpose beautifully for at least a year or two.

Another surprise: The best way to clean it is with water and a rag. Amazing!

## sourcing

**showerboard**
Showerboard is available in the bath fittings sections of home centers. Some of the national chains don't carry it, but local lumber suppliers often do. The d.school has had excellent results with the product available from Pine Cone Lumber (895 East Evelyn Avenue, Sunnyvale, CA 94086; 408 736-5491; www.pineconelumber.com). Reference "solid white tileboard" or "showerboard."

## see also

### 16
Tools_Z-Rack

### 58
Tools_Whiteboard Sliders

### 190
Tools_Writable Surfaces Everywhere

**top**
dimensions: 31 ½" x 31 ½"
(rolls through most doors)
material: 11-ply ¾" birch plywood

**removable box storage section**
dimensions (outer): 26" wide x 10" high x 15" deep
material: 11-ply ¾" birch plywood
(with single-side laminate)

**steel base**
dimensions: 26" wide (26" at base
tapering to 15" at top) x 24 ½" tall
material: 1½" square tube stock

# periodic
# table

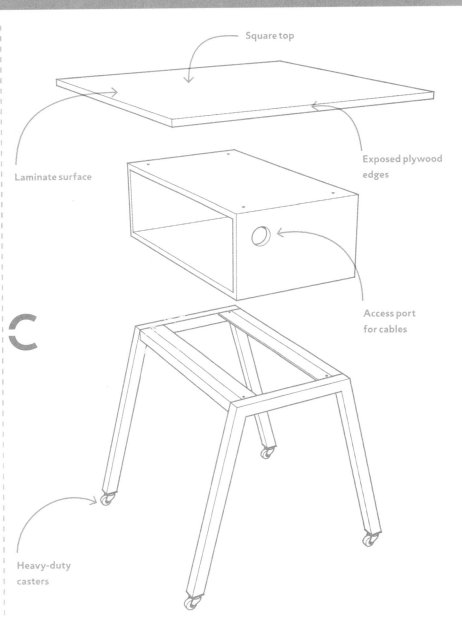

Square top

Exposed plywood
edges

Laminate surface

Access port
for cables

Heavy-duty
casters

# The Periodic Table redefines the role of a table in a team space. It's more cocktail party than conference—a place to pause and perch, a small part of a larger picture.

The Periodic Table is the core horizontal surface in the teaching spaces at the d.school: it is the carbon atom, the building block.

Groups of tables can be ganged together to create larger surfaces to suit different activities: in a row for a "buffet" configuration, in "L" shapes for group presentations, etc. The tables support a dynamic culture. Their composition of exposed ply-wood communicates a non-precious aesthetic—the tables are meant to be used and manipulated. Heavy-duty casters and a square top signal and allow easy reconfiguration, unlike most tables and desks.

The materials & dimensions are deliberately designed to encourage ac-tions and to promote cultural attitudes. At 39" tall with the storage box in place, the Periodic Table is more launchpad than anchor. The standard seating height for tables is around 29", while a "bar height" is around 40". The Periodic Table is deliberately in between those dimensions, with a bias toward the taller

height to help people transition from sitting to standing. The box section can be removed for longer, seated activities.

## sourcing

### tables
The Periodic Tables were constructed by Stan Heick at HCSI Manufacturing (16890 Church Street Building 7, Morgan Hill, CA 95037; phone 408 778-8231; www.hcsidesign.com).

### casters
The casters are from Industrial Caster & Wheel Co. (2200 Carden Street, San Leandro, CA 94577; phone 510 569-8303; www.icwco.com). Reference Stanford d.school red caster in 3" or 5".

## see also

### 24
Insights_Design with Multiple Situations in Mind

### 37
Insights_Expose Raw Materials

### 43
Design Template_Properties: Posture

### 60
Tools_Casters in Unexpected Places

## start

See Quick Component Tables (page 242) for ideas on how to quickly cobble together tables on the cheap. Make them standing height (39") and outfit them with square tops and casters.

Height: 29"
without box section

Height: 39"
with box section

# Start with What You Have.

see also

52
Design Template_Attitudes:
Bias toward Action

73
Insights_Don't Forget to Prototype

**Starting with what you have encourages you to start small, move quickly, invest less, be visible to others, and build momentum.**

**Creating a collaborative space is as simple as getting a space.**
A lot of energy and time can be wasted on overthinking where to start. Have an empty office, half of a warehouse, an empty conference room? Take it and transform it. Quickly. It will be hard to kick you out once you occupy the space—right or wrong—and it is hard to argue with proof of success. Display the way your space gets used; invite others to participate; become an example by working in the middle of your squatter's territory.

**Keep your space active by using it.**
Visible signs of use and activity can encourage others to participate. These traces of excitement also signal new ideas. Stagnant areas, piles of unused materials, and unattended corners and closets drag down the mood of a space.

# Building Your Own Space Is a Big Deal.

**Creating a space collaboratively is the best recipe for creating a collaborative space.**

This principle holds true for your whole community. Sharing opinions is the first step of participation in creating a space, but taking action and building the space provides another level of commitment and camaraderie. Furthermore, building a space for the first time builds momentum for the next iteration.

**The importance of actually building some aspect of your own space cannot be overstated.**
The act of "building"—whether that means cutting wood & building cabinets or selecting materials and furniture—connects you with the space as an invested owner rather than an entitled user.

see also

**136**
Insights_Help People Cope with Change

**176**
Insights_Recognize Your Emotional Arc during a Project

Faculty, staff, and volunteers building the walls within the first d.school building.

# around
# the campfire

**When curating the campfire activity, include seating choice & duration.**
Low, informal seating equalizes group eye level and comfort level. This seating position is unusual in Western culture; unlike an actual campfire engagement, this version is best kept relatively short.

**The "campfire" configuration can dramatically impact the quality of an activity.**
In the absence of actual flames, the posture & arrangement of people sitting around a fire (sitting low to the ground in a tight circle) heightens the awareness of group participants and the activity topic.

**Use the campfire for reflection and interpersonal sharing.**
The contrast between seated/standing height and low, squatting posture helps to ground the conversation. It feels safe, making the campfire a great way to debrief & address sensitive topics.

## start

At the end of your next activity, get rid of all of the seats in the room and try sitting in a low circle. Try low stools, the foam cube, or cardboard boxes, or simply sit on the floor.

## see also

18
Tools_Foam Cubes

43
Design Template_Properties: Posture

# photo booth

**The Photo Booth is a mini photo studio within your space.**
It should be a dark, acoustically isolated room with controllable lighting and space in which to set props & hang backdrops. The bigger the better, of course, but even a closet will do.

**Mobile-tech entrepreneur Akshay Kothari during a photo shoot in the d.school's Photo Booth.**

**The Photo Booth is a game-changer—instant media production is becoming an implicit expectation of corporate and student projects.**
Start-ups shoot their own product images, produce their own advertising, and own their communication. Major corporations resonate with the instant results of photos & demo videos that communicate real-time trends. Classes increasingly require multimedia deliverables.

Ideally, you'll need a fairly large room (12' x 24' or bigger), preferably with windows that don't face south (indirect sunlight is a wonderful lighting source) plus curtains to darken the room as needed.

Dig deeper, and seek advice from a pro or someone who is "in the know," to get beyond each of the Photo Booth starting points that follow.

**A camera and a tripod.**
Camera technology is ever in flux, but both video and still cameras are important to have. Digital SLRs have recently combined these functions into a single piece of equipment.

**An audio kit.**
Getting a microphone close to your subjects is critical. You'll need at least an external mic and a camera with an audio input.

**A lighting kit.**
Lighting is a key component of photography. We can't go into the nuances here, but it is a good idea to have at least a minimal set of lights with stands handy.

**A grip kit.**
Grip gear encompasses many things that work alongside lights but aren't electrical. This includes things like sandbags, stands, and reflectors.

**Backdrops.**
Simple white & black backdrops are great for visually separating out subjects for product shots and interviews.

**Paint.**
A warm, dark gray is a nice alternative to black. It absorbs light and adds a touch of always-welcome warmth.

**Soft surfaces.**
If you're not planning on doing much drilling into the floor, a dark, low-pile carpet is actually helpful to dampen echoes. To dampen echoes further, hang furniture pads on the walls, but use a neutral color like gray rather than blue.

## sourcing
Investigate professional photography and/or film and video stores in your local area.

## start

Start small, and get going. Take over a closet or curtain off part of a larger room. Make a sign announcing that this new resource is now available to everyone. Paint the walls, supply some basic equipment, and start shooting. Momentum will dictate the next steps: are you taking more product shots or shooting more "live-action" movies? The answer to this question will inform your direction and the next gear purchase.

## see also

52
Design Template_Attitudes: Show, Don't Tell

# Follow the Hacks: Innovation Is Everywhere.

**Pay attention to user-initiated changes and respond to them with modifications to your space.**

One of the best ways to develop a collaborative environment is to observe and amplify the ways in which your community already feels empowered to take control. If you care to notice, there is a tidal wave of tips and tricks in plain view at any instant in the form of hacks & work-arounds.*

Look and listen for anything being used unconventionally: How is a stack of chairs being used as a stepladder? Why is a smart phone being used as a presentation screen?

Every hack you uncover is an opportunity to design new ways of working in response: support emergent needs in technology & communication, rethink available resources, and empathize with the needs of your community.

*Jane Fulton Suri's book Thoughtless Acts (Chronicle Books, 2005) provides endless examples of these real-life work-arounds.

see also

**52**
Design Template_Attitudes: Focus on Human Values

**249**
Insights_It's about People

d.school students use Quick-Clamps to create improvised board storage.

Exterior finish of
a bungalow at the
Booneville Hotel,
Booneville, CA.
Designed & built by
the hotel's chef &
proprietor, Johnny
Schmitt, Studio128.

# Expose Raw Materials.

**Raw materials—such as wood, steel, concrete, glass, and leather—feel authentic and timeless. Lean toward exposing rather than concealing them.**

When you expose material, you expose structure and reveal how things are made. It's all there for the eye to see. Even in spaces that aren't about making physical objects, this visual accessibility communicates creative possibility.

Raw materials wear well. Like the natural environment from which they originate, they often grow more beautiful with a little patina. For the same reason, many raw materials—wood, in particular— generate a feeling of warmth. (This is not as true for glass & concrete, steel can go either way.)

Furniture that features raw materials often has less adornment. Less adornment = less styling. Less styling = more timeless.

Raw materials can be finished to feel less precious (of course, they can also be made to seem highly precious, as indeed they are). Less precious materials are approachable & malleable and can be a strong signifier for a culture of making.

Raw materials lend themselves more easily to experimentation: you can run a piece of wood through a table saw and cut it without chipping it, as you would with a laminate surface. You can also reuse raw materials in the next experiment. We've had a lot of fun with wood in that way—it's quite lovely.

## see also

# Space is the "body language" of an organization.*

Intentional or not, the form, functionality, and finish of a space reflect the culture, behaviors, and priorities of the people within it. This suggests that a space designer is simultaneously a cultural translator and a builder. That said, space design has its own grammar that can be tweaked to bolster desirable habits.

# Design Template_Introduction

This Design Template breaks down this spatial grammar into manageable bits. Use it as a guide to decipher the needs and opportunities presented by an existing space, or to design a completely new one. It should be as useful for working with an architect to conceive of a new building, as it is to figure how to repurpose a spare storage closet. Once you start to recognize and manipulate these pieces, you'll be amazed at what you can accomplish, even within modest means.

To focus and make it easier to start, the Design Template uses four specific categories: Places and Properties address the divisions in a space and the features within them; Actions and Attitudes address who is in the space and what they do.

## places

Places are broad spatial types that share an overall purpose.
(e.g., all spaces include Thresholds, such as doorways or openings, and Transitions, such as hallways.)

## properties

Properties are the specific aspects of people or space that can be enhanced or altered to impact behavior.
(e.g., personal posture can be drastically altered with seating modifications. Ambience attributes, such as lighting, can be used to elevate mood.)

## actions

Actions are behaviors and tasks.
(e.g., designers tend to visually saturate work spaces with project inspiration and artifacts.)

## attitudes

Attitudes are cultural values and habits.
(e.g., "Bias toward Action" is a core value at the d.school.)

With these four categories you can build dexterity into the process of creating new spaces and cultivating collaboration within your community. To further demonstrate these principles, we will share our personal experiences, offering them as examples for you to consider in your own work. †

*"Space is the 'body language' of an organization," comes to us from our colleague Chris Flink, of the d.school and IDEO. He claims it comes from elsewhere, but we have yet to find another valid source.

† The Design Template emerged from our collaboration with Adam Royalty and Dave Baggeroer at the d.school.

# 40

# places

Places are "zoning" for your space. Planning in broad zones rather overly detailed and specific rooms is an important first step in laying out a space designed to evolve. The trick is to define an area of use, then use minimal but meaningful semipermanent strokes (flooring choice, wall treatment, etc.) to define and support it. Consider behavior first and implementation second.

Thinking of places as zones that support behavior helps isolate underlying needs from conventional solutions, which often leads to novel and relevant innovations. This broader strategy also helps you consider the proportions of the particular spaces you'll need and helps you define adjacencies— which spaces are connected (and which are not).

We use four major "buckets" for identifying places that support behavior. There are overlaps in all categories—is a kitchen Support Structure or a Gathering Space? You will have to make the call as to how best to frame them within your culture. The key is to make sure you are covering all the bases.

**home base**
This is the principal place for individual or group creative work. Desks, offices, and project rooms are all Home Bases. Features include a designated place to create, display, and store work in progress.

**gathering spaces**
These are places people meet. A Gathering Space can be as obvious as a conference room, a lounge, a theater, or a classroom, or as subtle as a hallway outside of a lecture hall. Areas immediately adjacent to common tools often become Gathering Spaces—the spot next to a copy machine, or the proverbial watercooler.

**thresholds/transitions**
Thresholds are entry and exit points. Transitions are passages—like hallways. Both constitute the connective tissue that helps bind or separate activities and segue from one space to the next— outside to inside, in the case of a foyer. Thresholds and Transitions mark changes in mood, tempo, and subject matter as people move from space to space.

**support structure**
Support Structure is anything that supports and propels creative work, but has a "service" role. This includes storage rooms, resource rooms, kitchens, and so on. Planning with these places in mind helps ensure that support is well distributed throughout your space.

## home base

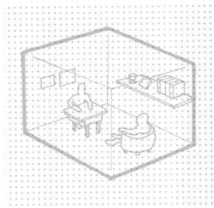

The Home Base is a physical or digital space where individuals or teams anchor their work and identity. From an emotional perspective, it is the creative center of gravity from which people advance and retreat. Whether you are a musician who calls the open road your home or a cold-calling salesperson perched at a desk for nine hours, the concept of a Home Base is still applicable. The manifestation of the details can be quite different, but the needs remain the same.

Most broadly, a Home Base has at least four attributes:
A place to access unique resources and tools
A place for things: persistent and accessible storage for work in progress
A place to showcase contributions: to display and share insights, work,

and practice

A place for a community to flourish: to share ideas, aspirations, and emotions, and to make connections

These attributes are starting points for challenging conventional work solutions such as offices, cubicles, and desks in order to identify how needs are actually met. Eliminating walls and doors to create a more visually linked community can be an exciting step in establishing a collaborative workplace. This does not however, remove the need for the sense of security and ownership that walls and doors provide. You will have to respond to these needs. For example, the d.school flanks its open office with several huddle rooms and personal hiding places to provide instant privacy when needed.

## gathering spaces

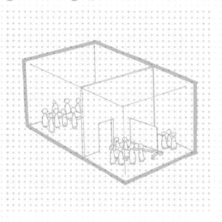

At the most fundamental evel, Gathering Spaces are where people meet. In a "normal" workplace Gathering Spaces might range from a kitchen to a conference room. Though activities within these spaces vary widely, the more responsible a person or group is for maintaining a space, the more flexible that space can be in responding to their needs. The predictability of a nonadjustable space makes it easy to drop in and out with little effort or expertise, while greater adjustability provides more options to an experienced user.

Consider the following categories of responsibility and adjustability when designing a Gathering Space. Note that, despite the focus on adjustability, all three have well-defined limits.

**Drop-in**
(e.g., laptop bar at a coffee shop)
These spaces can be effortlessly engaged and should virtually reset themselves. Bias toward fixed and predictable. Nothing should move except chairs.

**Curated**
(e.g., welcome area or lobby)
There might be some room for variation to liven things up, but these places are not usually reconfigured daily. These areas are prepped by the facility, not the person using the space.

**Self-Service**
(e.g., huddle room or event space)
These areas can be very flexible in order to be customized by users or support staff. Still, there should be a limited assortment of assets that are easy to use, with clear places to store them when done.

## thresholds/transitions

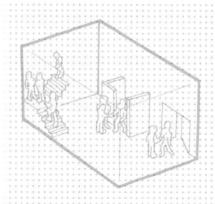

Thresholds and Transitions are in-between spaces. These often serve as boundaries between intended places and events. Because Thresholds and Transitions are ubiquitous, they play a surprisingly significant role in the overall experience of an environment.

Transitions are about movement & the moment. In any given activity, the first and last thing a participant experiences is a Transition. We move right through them, but Transitions paradoxically call attention to the moment. Hot towels on an airplane and previews at a movie theater are both examples of deliberate Transitional elements that signal a changing event. Physical space can be used in the same way.

Hallways, on-ramps, and lunch breaks are all different forms of Transitions. They are so common that they often do not stand out as details that need to be designed. It is a mistake to ignore the design of Transitions in a dynamic culture. Collaboration that shifts from one activity to the next and from one place to the next requires clear and direct support. Signage and way-finding cues are great starting points for designing Transitions.

Thresholds signify change, and they are easy opportunities for leveraging intuitive behaviors. People frequently expect to act differently when exiting one space and entering another. Children use playground voices outside; visitors (sometimes) remove their shoes before sitting down to dinner at friends' homes. Cultural behaviors around Thresholds are valuable assets to incorporate into spaces and activities. Don't shy away from calling attention to thresholds with bold visual strokes like changes in flooring or wall color.

## support structure

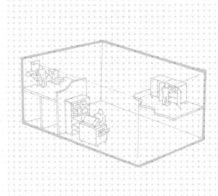

Support Structure includes a wide variety of spaces. As the somewhat generic name suggests, the only real requirement is that it support the actions and attitudes converging in adjacent spaces. A copy room supports the activities in a classroom, just as a prototyping room supports the attitude of biasing toward action. Typical examples of Support Structures are zones for utility areas—such as bathrooms and kitchens, closets, and service equipment.

Support Structures should always be considered in terms of location and quantity. To service the space well, you'll want them to be immediately at hand. When placing these spaces, consider both their position relative to other zones and the flow required to access them. Walk through some possible scenarios to determine whether you've got it in the right place. Imagine moving

supplies to and from a storage area to different parts of the space: what would it be like to walk to an upstairs kitchen carrying a case of wine?

We always need more space than we have, and Support Structures never really count as space for people or activities. Thus, they often end up underrepresented in the final floor plans. From storage to kitchens and bathrooms, more is almost always better. Resist the temptation to underserve the Support Structures—you'll just end up with a lot of junk out in the open where a closed storage area should be.

Think volume, not footprint. Like everything else, Support Structures don't need to be fixed. Storage in particular—via cabinets on wheels, like the Storage Towers (page 220)—can be moved throughout the space at will. Overhead rigging is another simple way to increase the usable volume for Support Structures.

# properties

Properties are spatial characteristics that can be used to transform behavior and mood. Each of these characteristics is adjustable and can be calibrated—on a scale, as in from "open" to "closed"—to radically alter the mood in a situation. These are simple and effective tweaks, and even a small change to a single property can fundamentally alter the nature of an interaction.

We use six different categories to help decipher actual behavior in an environment, as well as to help encourage (or discourage) which behaviors and moods might arise. Note that properties include features of the space itself as well as positions of the people within it.

**posture**
The physical positioning of the human body and the types of behaviors that position elicits.

**orientation**
The positioning of people and assets relative to each other.

**surface**
The orientation of work surfaces and planes within a space.

**ambience**
The atmospheric quality of an environment and its effect on the mood of an audience.

**density**
The size of a space relative to the activities and assets within it.

**storage**
The status of inactive objects.

## posture

 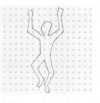

reflective ⟷ excited

Posture describes the position of a person's body in the midst of an activity. It signals and reinforces a spectrum of personal engagement ranging from reflective to active. Though there are plenty of counterexamples, it's fair to say that a reclined or seated posture suggests a reflective and relaxed engagement with an activity, whereas an upright or standing posture signals active engagement and participation. The study of work posture has often been concerned with minute changes in positioning to enhance the ergonomics of sitting at a desk for long periods. Instead, explore the richness of a wide range of postures—from standing to reclining—and you'll be rewarded with equally rich and purposeful shifts in collaboration patterns.

A reflective sitting posture, while comfortable, often disguises and diminishes the potential of body language and movement. It's static. We've noticed that the more comfortable people are in their seats, the less comfortable they seem to be with generating ideas, exchanging leadership roles, or moving on to the next activity. As a result, reflective posture is great for critique and reflection, but bad for generating ideas. For the same reasons, however, it works well for team debriefs and deep discussions.

An active, standing posture encourages people to jump in and alter the dynamics of a room. This posture also leaves room for fidgeting and stretching to release tension. Like it or not, our body language communicates intent & emotion, and we negotiate comfort level & status relationships through our proximity to each other. Use active posture to tap into these deep communication channels by making it easy for everyone to get up, move, and sit down again.

## orientation

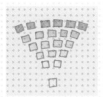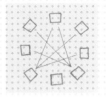

singular ←——————————→ multifaceted

"Orientation" is the relative positioning of people and assets. "Singular" directs all attention on a single person (e.g., a teacher) or object (e.g., a prototype). "Multifaceted" highlights all things equally: imagine a group sitting in a circle—no single person is the focus.

Orientation is often the principal vehicle for directing visual attention and tuning human connection within an experience. It is also one of the easiest properties to manipulate because in many cases it requires only adjusting the direction in which people are standing or sitting. In other situations, orientation may be less variable, though no less important, due to preexisting boundaries or furniture.

Orientation illuminates one of the fundamental differences between a fixed-furniture and an adjustable environment. During highly focused activities such as a class or a classical music performance, the orientation of the audience is often singularly focused on the source of the sight and sound. The arrangement of furniture reflects the desired engagement between source and audience: rows of fixed seats facing forward. In a contrary situation where the intent is to have participants see, hear, and engage each other, an open, multifaceted orientation is preferable. In these latter cases, furniture that allows movement and adjustability is key.

## surface

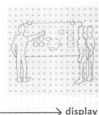

create ←——————————→ display

Surface describes the planes that teams and individuals work on—are people using desks, tables, walls, or floors to create or display their work?

Simple changes in surface orientation can have profound impact: horizontals generally support individual authoring, while verticals put work on display for groups. Many people are accustomed to creating work on small, individual-sized panels like desks, laptop computers, or notebooks. More often than not, these surfaces are horizontal, creating a fairly private or hidden environment. Transitioning from a horizontal work surface to a vertical one enhances collective visibility, but it is often contrary to the norms people associate with "doing work."

"Create" surfaces can be horizontally or vertically mounted (or somewhere in between) and should take on many shapes and characters, depending on circumstances. Surfaces for building wood prototypes using power tools and adhesives will be fundamentally different from surfaces for performing surgery or for painting a canvas. In general, bias toward as large as possible for any building spaces in order to leave work unbounded and easily accessible.

Display surfaces are often vertical, but they can be horizontal, too. The context informs the configuration. Teammates, working together and sharing information with others, often display their work on vertical surfaces to make information immediately visible to anyone within the line of sight. Display surfaces should also be large, but often must be portable and reusable, suggesting lightweight and durable panels such as foamboard.

## ambience

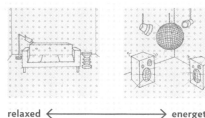

relaxed ⟵⟶ energetic

Ambience describes the more ethereal features of an environment: lighting, textures, sounds, smells, and color. Think of it as an expression of emotional tone. Adjustments can be tailored to elicit different emotional responses from those occupying the space.

Ambience is a magical tool in that people experience it fully but don't always notice it explicitly. Creating the right ambience is a highly nuanced art form, but a couple of rules of thumb can get you started. For relaxed spaces, go with plush seating, multiple points of light, quiet music, and warm or dark colors. For active spaces, try raw materials, bright light, bouncy music, saturated colors, and open windows.

## density

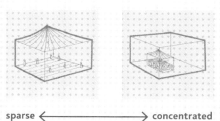

sparse ⟵⟶ concentrated

Density characterizes how a volume of space feels in relation to an activity. Tweaking density allows you to influence these impressions and control the energy level and creative potential of an experience. A sparse environment provides ample interpersonal distance in which people feel free to move about and might feel more self-reflective. A concentrated environment engages participants closely within a "cozier" space.

The paradox of density is that both sparse and concentrated spaces can achieve similar results: an empty space such as a large, vacant studio can create the perfect platform for creativity, and a concentrated environment packed with contact points and stimuli can be equally effective. Some people head to the desert for inspiration; others prefer New York City. You can resolve this paradox by homing in on the specific activity of the person or team. If the activity is about realizing or making things, perhaps a sparse studio with plenty of open space will provide physical and mental room for building. If the activity involves absorbing inspiration from many stimuli or maintaining a collective energy, a concentrated environment saturated with images, sounds, and other people will do.

Separate the quality of Density from the size of a space—its physical dimensions—in order to focus on the intent of an experience. The key is to tune the feeling of energy in a space by packing it full or leaving it sparse, no matter its size. Strategic positioning of furniture & room dividers can make a large space feel concentrated even with a small number of people. Purging a room or removing a dropped ceiling can make a smaller space feel sparse.

## storage

protected ←——————————→ available

Storage is about accessibility of both artifacts and information. It spans the range from protected—accessible only to those who know its secrets—to available, out in the open, and shared. Accessibility of storage is an important issue for digital and physical resources. The same considerations given to placement of a file cabinet or bookshelf apply to servers, memory cards, and cloud accounts.

Security is important, but it must be balanced with the visibility necessary in a collaborative context. Bias toward keeping materials and work easily accessible in a creative space unless they absolutely must be protected. This strategy will find you accessing storage far more frequently and purposefully, to the point where storage itself becomes an active work space.

The ability to store things in a space also links to how that space is experienced. Storage and security are directly related to the concept of a Home Base (page 40) or a place that people feel they can control. Giving someone

storage resources can be a meaningful gesture of community connectedness. Likewise, a policy of "no storage" sends a different strong message.

Whether protected or available, storage is often underestimated in the design and support of creative spaces. This is true in most spaces, actually, as evidenced by the nearly sexual appeal of an apartment with large closets. Creating a collaborative environment in which materials are available and encouraged for use requires actually storing those materials. It also potentially requires maintaining a buffer or back-stock of materials. In general, it's important to allocate plentiful and prominent space for storage, or else objects will find a way to be stored in unlikely and undesirable places.

# actions

Arranging an environment to incite and
support specific behaviors is precisely
the intent of space design. Simply identifying the activity you are in or about to
begin can help design a space suited to
that purpose.

Actions are the different steps of
"doing" at any given moment. The six
different activities identified here are
basic descriptions of what someone
might be doing during a snapshot in
time. They arise from the d.school's
particular brand of creative process, but
they are broad enough to be transfer-
rable to other working styles. Borrow
them entirely, pick and choose parts of
them, or lead with actions of your own.

### saturate
This is the unloading and sharing of
information and ideas. Implicit in
saturation is revealing and displaying
information—often through stories,
photos, illustrations, and graphs.

### synthesize
This process involves creating clarity from complexity. Synthesis
often requires taking a lot of available
information and combining, omitting,
and rearranging elements to generate a
new way of framing a problem.

### focus
Narrowing on a single topic or task for a
sustained period requires the personal
discipline to ignore other activities and
topics. Focusing is an important part of
working toward an insight or implementing an idea.

### flare
Going big with ideas by generating tons
of new concepts and options. Flaring
often requires ignoring constraints
and suspending disbelief in favor of
creating something new. Brainstorming,
or ideating, is a common way to
flare. Daydreaming potential solutions
is another.

### realize
Turning an idea or concept into
something tangible. Building prototypes
is an example of realization: the activity
moves beyond simply talking about
an idea to creating something that can
actually be evaluated or shipped.

### reflect
Reconsideration of what just happened.
The intents of reflection are to learn, illuminate, capture, and evaluate aspects
of past events and how they can impact
what is yet to come. In many cases,
reflection is an activity that signals a
next step, not necessarily an endpoint.

## saturate

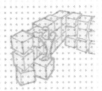

Saturation is a process for inspiration. A saturated space is mindfully curated to display and broadcast information, express emotion, and immerse a team in the environment of a problem. People instinctively decorate spaces with artifacts and attributes from other places or experiences—family photos on a work desk, a car's rearview mirror strung with a graduation tassel, etc. The trick is to transform a neutral space—such as an office, classroom, or conference room—into one that displays the attributes of another space or experience that is critical to your design.

Photographs, quotes, and artifacts are excellent materials for saturating a space. Imagine that a research team conducts a series of customer interviews to investigate how a product is actually being used. Following those interviews, the research team retreats into a work space to "unpack" all of the information. Saturating could include displaying photographs of the interviewees, sketches of ideas that came up during the interviews, juicy quotes, and a physical example or two of the product being discussed. Being

surrounded by all this material helps a team recall pertinent details that may be keys to a new, authentic idea.

Employ quick methods for display to make saturation easy. Post-its and Sharpies are effective tools for capturing and displaying quotes on walls, windows, and dry-erase surfaces. Painter's tape is extremely handy for posting pictures and sheet material on vertical surfaces without destroying the finish. Digital cameras and portable printers provide the kind of instant visualization that space saturation requires. Digital projectors are useful for creating immediate slideshows to pan through images of an event.

Think ahead. Part of the magic of re-creating an experience is mindfully capturing these inspirational photos, quotes, video, and audio on the fly.

## synthesize

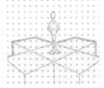

Patterns, trends, themes, and hidden mysteries . . . this is the stuff of synthesis. Synthesis is about grabbing data from a pile of assorted facts and details, and rearranging data in various ways to create meaning or a strong direction.

Before synthesis, people will

walk into a room with a bunch of facts and concepts they "know." Following synthesis, these same people will walk out of a room understanding what their knowledge actually means. In between is a messy task involving unpacking data and ideas and recombining them into new insights. This is a big shift, and a difficult task, but it is the often unacknowledged foundation of innovation!

The environment supporting synthesis should be as flexible as the minds at work! Synthesis often challenges people to start with a blank mind, build up a complex perspective, tear that down, and begin again. The ability to visualize, sort, and re-sort data and insights is important. Large, blank vertical surfaces coupled with tools for display and rearrangement can help create a fertile synthesis zone. As with saturation, reconfigurable tools such as Post-its and dry-erase surfaces are very helpful. This approach toward visualizing thoughts, or thinking spatially, can have a profound effect on the discovery of hidden patterns and details "between thoughts."

Mindmapping and storyboarding are two excellent tools for synthesis. In his book Experiences in Visual Thinking (Brooks/Cole, 1973), Stanford Professor Emeritus Bob McKim suggests visually arranging thoughts, topics, and sequences for both individual work and teamwork. Grouping elements can identify themes and illuminate transitions. Filmmakers have long used storyboards to highlight action and plan transitions from one scene to the next. Pixar Studios is notable for having huge storyboards prominently on display during the development of their animated films. This helps synchronize and synthesize their work.

## focus

Focus is narrowing on a single topic or task. It is the art of letting go: what you decide not to do is as important as what you are doing. In some instances letting go means abandoning something completely, and in other cases it means setting it aside temporarily. In either case, focusing is a critical step in distilling information rather than diluting it.

Focus requires intentionality. A helpful question to ask is: "Are we seeking new ideas and new information at this point or are we homing in on an answer?" For example, after a really productive brainstorming session, a team might be confronted with the task of evaluating hundreds of ideas. In this case, the next step in work is to evaluate a few ideas by testing them. In many ways, evaluating an idea is precisely the opposite of generating new ideas.

Acknowledging the shift from idea generation to idea evaluation helps things move more smoothly. There is always more work that can be done, but focusing on a specific aspect or phase of the work benefits overall progress.

## flare

Flaring is a phase for exploring possibilities and generating options. At the beginning of a project cycle, flaring might include a wide and divergent effort to understand what is going on in the world around the project space. Late in a project, it might include generating multiple options to explore potential solutions.

Flaring often includes brainstorming and other techniques for idea generation. Just as with the intent of brainstorming, flaring explicitly includes generating and receiving new information around a particular topic in order to move beyond the known and obvious, toward the new and novel.

Suspend disbelief for the sake of getting somewhere new and unexplored. Stay on topic, but save judgment for later. The goal in flaring is to generate options so you have some material

to work with when you get to a decision point. If thoughts and concepts outside of your topic space arise, it's important to accept them and move on. Brilliant ideas can be saved and addressed at a later time. Although it may seem like a paradox, staying on topic can be a helpful method for breaking new ground.

## realize

Realization is the process of making the ethereal tangible. It's the difference between saying that you like to paint and finishing a painting. Realization can involve many different actions: programming code, drafting business plans, and making mock-ups or models. Regardless of medium or method, most important is the simple step of actually doing something.

Iterate: build, then discuss. Then build on top of that. Let your realization become a touchstone for discussion, rather than the other way around. Build first, think later.

How you realize has a huge impact on the kind of space you will need, but some things remain constant. Building an interface for a database requires a much different space than building an irrigation system for a farm. That said, realization always requires storage for work in progress, room to expand and experiment, space to show and share, and a place to focus. The nature and quantity of these things can change depending on what and how you are realizing. (Storage for digital work may be housed on a server, while physical prototypes require shelving.) But make no mistake: space to gather and work physically is important for even the most ethereal digital project, even digital game designers use physical prototypes to work out ideas.

project, explicitly build in check-in points where team members can voice initial reactions to the work or the activity. At times this might feel forced or slightly awkward, but with increased practice at quick and honest reflection, you'll find the sessions increasingly fruitful.

## reflect

Reflection is often seen as a conclusion, but really it is a highly dynamic, transitional activity. Reflection is best approached with an open mind and a learner's bias. Insights culled from mistakes—there are always mistakes—are helpful in preparing for the future, but dissecting what went "right" is every bit as helpful and informative.

Getting in touch with your team is as valuable as digging into your work. Reflect in real time. During a team activity or over the course of a sustained

# attitudes

Shaping attitudes and the behaviors they inspire is the "holy grail" of space design.

Our attitudes steer our decisions and build momentum in everything we do. A space is at its most sublime when it reinforces and encourages desired values. Instilling attitudes also happens to be the trickiest part of designing a space, as attitudes are hard to predict, even harder to force and enforce, and harder still to measure. Nevertheless, a space that shapes attitudes is worth seeking—and you'll know when it's working.

The first step in designing a space to support particular attitudes is to define those attitudes. Because this step is a bit abstract, don't get too hung up on it. Different organizations have various ways to express core values and decision-making rubrics. As an example, the d.school uses the following six attitudes, called mindsets, in defining the basis of its culture. These attitudes strike a balance between being comprehensive yet still actionable. They are also robust enough to be defended, but not so precious that they can't be reevaluated. Don't shy away from altering these or your own values. Commit to them, but as with the space, leave room for them to evolve as you continue to learn.

**collaborate across boundaries**
Mix people with varied backgrounds and perspectives to launch your work into new and unexpected territories.

**show, don't tell**
Embody your work as quickly as you can so that others can interact with it. Don't spend your time "hand-waving"—you can create something just as quickly.

**bias toward action**
Do something first. Talk and think about it later.

**focus on human values**
Let people and the insights you develop from your interactions with them inspire your work. Design work benefits from providing for others, not inflating your ego.

**be mindful of process**
Recognize what you are trying to accomplish at any given moment and hold off on other activities until the time is right, but ultimately make sure to cover all your bases.

**prototype toward a solution**
Progress quickly and incrementally on the way to an end goal. Make your ideas tangible and frequently test them with others. Work at a low resolution to avoid heavy expenses early on.

## collaborate across boundaries

Collaboration among individuals from different disciplines can make the difference between innovative and conventional solutions. Often, innovative ideas can be found in the cracks between current domain definitions. Bringing together people with wildly different backgrounds increases the likelihood of stumbling on these useful intersections.

Keep in mind that as people work together on common problems, their approaches may vary greatly. Multidisciplinary teams—groups of people with different core talents and capabilities—can fail if misunderstanding trumps collective effort. Communication is essential in buoying the remarkable power of multiple perspectives.

Teams need support. Collaboration may not be an instinctive approach within your culture. As you shift toward this type of working style, make it okay for people to address interpersonal issues that arise around their work. Asking participants to share their states of mind as a group is a great first step in demonstrating that teamwork is important and valued.

Collaboration is not a prescription for "design by committee." Bring in multiple perspectives to fitness-test concepts, but leave decision making to a small team.

Effective storytelling with a "show, don't tell" attitude means conveying ideas through details rather than conjecture, being as concise as possible in communicating a meaningful transformation, and using authentic emotional tension to build empathy in your audience.

You must pay attention. In the thrill of the unknown are lots and lots of little details that, if noticed, will validate any effort to try something new. Pay attention afterward as well; reflection on what you did is key to a deeper understanding of the problem.

## show, don't tell

A "show, don't tell" attitude means creating compelling visuals and tangible artifacts to enable participants to experience the context of the challenge. Got an idea about what it would it be like to have a classroom without desks? Don't discuss it; demonstrate it, by removing all the desks and holding an actual class. Creating an experience will reveal details that may not be obvious in conversation and illuminate details that could not have been foreseen.

As a design becomes more resolved, the "show, don't tell" attitude applies in a different context—story telling. Perhaps you have had the unfortunate experience of listening to a friend or colleague aimlessly recount the details of a mundane event. When the end of the story came, how did you feel? Do you even remember the point?

## bias toward action

"Just do it," Nike's classic ad campaign, is consistent with the attitude of biasing toward action. Taking action and trying something new are not at odds with careful consideration of intent and outcome. The trick is not to let intent and outcome get in the way of exploring the unknown. There's always a reason not to do—people can and will rationalize a way out of doing anything. Biasing toward action depends on not necessarily knowing what will come next but being willing to try something to precisely determine what works and what does not.

Action does not overshadow thinking. Trying something simply for the sake of trying it can be exciting, but in the context of designing toward solutions and expanding the potential for innovation, you have to pay attention.

## focus on human values

Focusing on human values requires you to challenge your own beliefs in an effort to engage and understand others. This often means squelching the natural tendencies of the ego. One of the most difficult things to do in focusing on human values is to just shut up and listen. As ridiculous as that sounds, it is actually hard to do. Taking design cues from a user rather than having to blindly project a solution is surprisingly liberating—each user is like an added team member helping to inform the design. Neat trick!

Human values–focused design is not user-led, but it is insight-driven. Individual interactions with users can provide valuable inspiration and insights, but they are not prescriptions to be followed at face value. They still need to be synthesized with other factors into a final design, by the designers.

There is tension in deriving a solution based on an existing need versus creating a need for a particular product. There are many examples of great products and innovations that fall into both categories, but in the context of an infinitely large pool of challenges, a systematic approach focusing on human values, tendencies, and behaviors often better supports a designer's own intuition. The alternative—that an individual designer intrinsically has the perfect solution for any given person, at any given moment—is far less likely.

## be mindful of process

It is important to view your current actions and environment in the scope of larger contexts. Much of design is an immediate and reactive experience that requires myopic intensity at given moments. Being mindful of process means paying close attention to how you work, then making alterations to your work plan as needed. Even one change can affect many systems, so it's important to be aware of the implica-tions: How is your team responding to an event? What will it mean to try

something again? Can you afford not to try something again?

Being mindful of process does not equate to playing it safe. In fact, it might be the most counterintuitive attitude there is, leading directly, and knowingly, into failure! Failure, in the contexts of business, budgets, and timelines often translates to danger. However, in being truly mindful of process you can achieve a balance between knowing that you are going to fail and the fact that the anticipated failure will make the next step more productive and lead to better results. This is often true in the case of prototyping, where the goal is not necessarily the success of the prototype itself but the depth of the learning it provides.

## prototype toward a solution

Prototyping toward a solution requires fundamental behaviors: taking creative leaps; creating experiences and artifacts expressly to be tested; leveraging the lowest-resolution resources necessary to explore a concept; accepting feed-back as delivered, then making sense of it in the context of additional feedback;

and cycling through multiple iterations of a concept early and often.

Prototypes are not precious, but the lessons you glean from them are. Prototyping is the act of making in service of learning: the goal is to learn the most with the least. The resolution of the things you make should match the resolution of your ideas about the problem you are solving. Early on, ideas and concepts are often at their fuzzi-est—meaning that the aspects needing validation are still highly abstract. Rather than spend tremendous amounts of money, time, and opportunity, use quick, low-resolution tests before homing in on more refined concepts. Similarly, begin with a large pool of prototypes to explore options and narrow down as your solution becomes resolved over time & testing.

# TED:
# The Environment Designed

## by Frank Graziano

# Space Studies_TED: The Environment Designed

When the researchers and designers at Steelcase were first invited to create the environment for the annual three-and-a-half-day gathering for TED (Technology, Entertainment, and Design), we began by asking ourselves: How might we create compelling experiential spaces in this temporary environment? Our challenge stemmed from the tension in designing for a temporal venue, given what we know and have observed in other contexts. The excitement came from both weaving together the five fundamental principles discussed here and ultimately understanding how people engage activities and their surroundings as a result.

## 1. Being mindful of the greater context

At TED, the eighteen-minute presentations (TEDTalks) are held live in an auditorium and also simultaneously broadcast in multiple adjacent spaces, which allows attendees to balance a full immersion in the content while conversing and socializing.

We crafted a network of places specifically intended to connect people based on their different behaviors. There is a bookstore, several locations for coffee and tea, and many alcoves and different zones that people may choose. Some of the simulcast spaces offer large screens and lounge seating, supporting informal groups watching together. In others, the simulcasts are presented as a tool with whiteboards, pens, paper, and phones, allowing attendees to come together to think, create, and engage with each other.

top: The macro and micro environments of the TED experience.

bottom: Environments designed for laptops, lounges, and lectures.

### 2. Planning spaces
### for varied learning styles

Artists, actors, and writers as well as scientists, mathematicians, and business leaders gather at TED. They are drawn by the opportunity to connect with others who hold common beliefs and goals.

We took into account a variety of learning styles while creating the overall campus venue. Auditory learners might listen to the simulcast while wandering through the bookshop, but visual learners might want to be in the dimly lit theater setting to attain the greatest focus. Bloggers and note takers were given dedicated areas so that the tapping of keys wouldn't disturb those who preferred to watch and listen in silence. Finally, there was theater-style seating accompanying round tables for attendees who desired a more traditional learning experience.

### 3. Accommodating
### and accelerating transitions

The programming of TED is intentionally social. Forty-five-minute breaks throughout the day allow one to digest the content of the lectures, refresh, and socially connect with others while getting a drink or snack.

To harness the energy of this constant rhythm of people moving about, the paths and interstitial spaces were developed with intentional views and vistas. The sight lines from one setting to another created a feeling of being a part of something much greater. The open views encouraged stroll-up conversations—recognizing someone from a distance, then approaching to make connection. Seating was offered at different heights: stools allowed for perching and taking in the sights, while lower lounge seating encouraged a variety of relaxed and intimate postures.

### 4. Using ambiguity
### as an invitation

TED itself already has settings that have become iconic to its brand—for example, TED beds and beanbags. Though the utility of these objects is clear, their presence in the context of a conference is a surprise—it invites people to reframe their expectations of what is "appropriate" behavior.

We employed this principle in subtle ways as we designed each environment. By adding a layer of props that were slightly incongruous, we introduced and welcomed new patterns and behaviors. Ultimately, those who used the space assigned to it a new meaning.

## 5. Fostering a sense of belonging

Over the course of the three-and-a-half days, participants establish routines within the conference environment. We actively sought out ways to encourage them to feel ownership of the place.

Integrating elements that were easily manipulated or controlled by the participants—such as lighting, spatial dividers, or movable carts—enabled individuals and small teams to establish a home base or camp. These elements were intuitive in their purpose and asked for users to "adopt" them. Because these elements were repeated throughout the entire space, participants felt a greater sense of belonging and mastery of the environment rather than staking out a single corner for the duration of the event.

Frank Graziano is Principal Researcher at Steelcase. His research and designs focus on emergent patterns and trends in human interactions.

Lights, seating, and sound augment the audience experience.

Sliders are a cheap and flexible way to define an open studio space.

Balance width with weight—30" wide is pretty good.

2"–4" gap at the floor—enough for a steadying sneaker

Add a runner at the bottom to stabilize while writing.

# whiteboard sliders

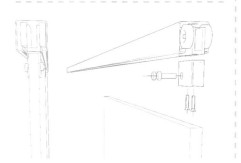

Dynamic & deployable dry-erase surfaces can transform a space from a warehouse to a series of studios and back again in seconds. They instantly create partitions & provide plenty of writing surface. At their most basic level, they are simply panels attached to trolleys that travel along rails.

Construction details can vary: size of panel, type of trolley, length of channel, ceiling/truss for mounting. Basic panels are cheap and simple to build using showerboard adhered to both sides of a plywood backing. Corrugated polycarbonate is another excellent option as a lightweight, translucent dry-erase surface.

It is best to enlist an engineer or facilities professional to refine the weight and attachment details. Check out your rail-mounting options: attaching directly to the ceiling structure, attaching to trusses, mounting to wall studs, or hanging from a threaded rod that is attached to the ceiling structure. Measure your floor-to-ceiling height and subtract the hardware dimensions to get the dimensions for your panel materials. Source your panels and hardware: laminate first, then cut to final size, and drill some attachment holes. Connect the trolleys and install panels in the rails. Slide away!

## tips

· Try to make individual runs as long as you can—seams can cause bumps in the trolley run as the building shifts. Unistrut rails are are often sold in runs of 20'. "Barn door" tracks and trolleys are an elegant alternative.

· If you are using a Unistrut C-shaped channel for the rail, make sure mounting screws are flush inside the channel and/or use brackets to mount threaded rod outside the channel. You'll need the space inside the channel to enable the trolley to move.

## sourcing

### panels
The d.school currently uses custom slider panels developed in collaboration with Steelcase. Simple panel materials (plywood & showerboard) can be sourced from local lumber yards and home centers. A local source in the San Francisco Bay Area is Pine Cone Lumber (895 East Evelyn Avenue, Sunnyvale, CA 94086; 408 736-5491; www.pineconelumber.com). Reference "solid white tileboard" or "showerboard."

### rails and trolleys
The d.school currently uses $1^5/_8$"-wide Unistrut channel (Part P1000). Standard Unistrut trolleys (Part P2949 & Part P2750) are versatile and easy to install. Unistrut (www.unistrut.com) offers steel materials with many standard connection options. Unistrut in the San Francisco Bay Area: Lord & Sons (430 East Trimble Road, San Jose, CA 95131; 800 468-3791; www.lordandsons.com).

## start

Prototype slider quantities & locations at full scale using cardboard or foamboard. The next steps are to consult appropriate facilities professionals to figure out how to proceed with installation, check out the rail-mounting options, calculate the dimensions and acquire sourcing panels, assemble the panels, install the hardware, and mount your sliders.

80/20 is another commercially available option consisting of aluminum materials with many precision function options: 80/20 Inc. (1701 South 400 East, Columbia City, IN 46725; www.8020.net).

## see also

hack

Casters are revolutionary: they will change your space.

casters in
unexpected places

One of the most unintentionally iconic elements of the d.school is a red couch on casters. The first couch was a "decadent" IKEA purchase made just after the d.school was getting its legs. The idea of putting the couches on casters was born out of the necessity of constantly reconfiguring the teaching environment in the earliest d.school building (Birch Hall). Birch had only one teaching space, and as a result it was constantly being rearranged.

Couches on casters revealed a cultural characteristic: the expectation & need to rapidly reconfigure dependable infrastructure. This led to experimentation with casters on other items that you wouldn't expect, such as walls.

While it might seem cheeky to have couches with wheels (they are often seen cruising around the space), the fact that casters in unconventional places can readily transform an environment is the real reason to celebrate them. As an example, the couches both create comfortable, intimate gathering spaces for teams and enable speedy transformation of a space to service another activity.

## build instructions:

Putting casters on most items is as simple as it seems, but keep two nonobvious things in mind:

1. Buy & install the best casters you can afford— there is nothing worse than having to move a couch on wheels only to discover that the wheels don't work.

2. Be sure to determine how you will attach the casters before you order or buy them. Casters can be ordered with a variety of connection plates and rods.

## sourcing

### couches
The red couches we use and abuse are called Klippan and come from IKEA (www.ikea.com). They are available in colors other than red, like black.

### casters
Industrial Caster & Wheel Co. (2200 Carden Street, San Leandro, CA 94577; 510 569-8303; www.icwco.com). Reference Stanford d.school red caster in 3" or 5".
California Caster and Hand Truck Company (1400 17th Street, San Francisco, CA 94107; 800 950-8750; www.californiacaster.com)
McMaster-Carr (600 North County Line Road, Elmhurst, IL 60126; 630 600-3600; www.mcmaster.com)

## start

Attach casters to an item that you already have. Choose something that you would not expect to have casters: a couch, an ottoman, or a large table. See if it encourages you to experiment with new configurations.

## see also

24
Insights _Design with Multiple Situations in Mind

100
Situations_Anchors

# prototyping room

**Want to cultivate a "maker" culture? Support the attitude of building with the space and tools to do it.**
An area for prototyping can be as modest as a co-opted closet or as elaborate as a machine shop. The details of the space are not as important as the broad strokes of providing quick access to resources and surfaces for working.

**Keep tools for shaping and joining on display and within reach.**
Tools for cutting and connection are critical: handsaws, blade tools, and scissors pair well with staplers, hot-melt glue guns, and power drills.

**start**

Co-opt a room or closet and set up a 6'-long table. A standard folding table is fine for light activity, sawhorses and a piece of $^3/_4$" plywood can help with slightly heavier-duty work. Mount some wall hooks and set up a toolbox. Put up a sign declaring the intent and availability of your new space. As space, time, and funding become available, keep expanding it.

**Make your space accessible.**
Announce your space with a sign and a "drop in anytime" access policy. You might find you have to balance the noise of innovation with the silence of the status quo.

**see also**

49
Design Template_Actions: Realize

53
Design Template_Attitudes: Prototype toward a Solution

**Electrical power and raw materials are equally important.**
Support the tools you provide with the power they require: place outlets everywhere and battery chargers in the open. Keep on hand a stock of raw materials, including sheet materials such as wood, cardboard, and foamboard. Provide ready access to an assortment of connection resources: screws, staples, hinges, and tape.

**Uninterrupted work surfaces are critical.**
Prototyping requires physical exploration and constructive mess making. Provide as many surfaces as your space will allow, while leaving room to maneuver around them. Keep in mind that the floor is a work surface, too: concrete floors and non-precious finishes support an "it's okay to build here" mentality.

# Seek Inspiration from Unexpected Locations.

**Inspiration is everywhere;
keep your eyes open all the time.**

Are you trying to create an ambience that makes people feel comfortable while they are conversing? That booth you are sitting in at the local diner might be the solution. Or are you trying to come up with just the right welcoming

experience for your space? You might find the answer in your church (divine inspiration, anyone?).

**Get curious.**
Whatever excites you is right. Follow that impulse & let yourself go. Some of the most inspired ideas are prompted by spaces that, on the surface, seem unrelated to the problem at hand. We've found course-altering inspiration for classrooms in kitchens and soundstages. Worry about what makes sense later.

**Align with your intent.**
Sometimes stealing solutions outright feels appropriate from the start and works great in the end—the light fixture

at that nightclub might just provide the perfect vibe for a new meeting space. Other solutions are more inspirational; they have some elements that fit your space but shouldn't be applied directly— something about the ambience of that spa felt right, but terrycloth robes and lavender massage oil aren't appropriate amenities in your new lounge area. Dig in a bit and identify the aspect that can be translated into the culture you mean to create. Is it the contrast between the spa environment and the outside world that seems like it would be a plus for your culture? Is it the use of natural materials that catches your eye?

**Capture & broadcast your insights.**
Whether your mobile technology is a camera or a sketchbook, capture images and thoughts as you cover your bases. Do whatever works for you and helps you to dig a bit deeper later. Then, surround yourself with evidence of this inspiration by saturating your project room or office with the visuals & notes.

## see also

**43**
Design Template_Properties

**48**
Design Template_Actions: Saturate

**66**
Insights_Define Your Intent

**The d.school's
Periodic Table:
dynamic & modular.**

**U.S. Navy
linemen poised
for play.**

# Separate Needs from Solutions.

**Avoid conventional solutions by isolating the needs at play then solving for each in its own way.**

Unlike a closed door, a semi-permeable screen helps individuals focus without ignoring the need to see what is going on elsewhere.

Consider the personal office. It is a solution to a host of needs: it's a place to store your things, it's a place where you feel a sense of territory and belonging, it can serve to signify your status in the organization, and it's a place in which to focus on work. Accepting and implementing the office as the only solution for all of these needs leads to the standard, inflexible honeycomb of offices and cubicles.

Separate these needs from one another, and you create fertile ground for innovation with a broader set of solutions that might be better suited to your particular culture or the culture you are hoping to develop. Status could be signified through social norms—or maybe it should be done away with altogether. Focus on work might be accomplished in any number of specialized or temporary spaces, each tailored to a particular type of work.

## see also

### 36
Insights_Follow the Hacks:
Innovation Is Everywhere

### 52
Design Template_Attitudes:
Focus on Human Values

Not quite a tent and not quite a Land Rover in Evje, Norway.

# Define Your Intent.

**Know what you want to get from each space, articulate it, and act on it.**

Some designers refer to point of view, while many architects use the term parti to describe an organizing principle for a space. No matter what you call it, creating a concise guiding statement for your spaces helps you make detail decisions.

As an example, the d.school has a relaxation room called Booth Noir:

"Booth" describes the size and use case—it's a private space for one or two people—and "Noir" describes the intent—it's a calm counterpoint to the hyper-extroverted energy in the rest of the workplace.

**Helpful hints for honing a guiding concept:**

**Use metaphors.**
Metaphors work really well to encapsulate ideas. "This is a 'home' for creative work." The word home is loaded with meaning that can guide your design.

**Make it sexy, short, and specific.**
You're looking to capture big themes in a sticky little package that you can use to tee up your ideas later.

**Allude to specific users and insights.**
The way a visitor experiences the space is going to be different from the way someone who works there uses it—guiding concepts should respond to specific users and use cases.

**Consider multiple scales.**
It's important to do this for the entire space (e.g., the building, floor, or suite) and the rooms within it. The building level will help guide big decisions about how people who work in the space feel ("it's my workshop") and how visitors experience it (surprises around every corner). On the room scale these concepts will help you amplify the attributes of each space to service specific needs well (e.g.: This classroom is an Instant Studio for teams).

**Commit and let go.**
Guiding concepts are benchmarks for building momentum but can morph as you dig deeper and better understand how the design of your space should unfold.

## see also

48
Design Template_Actions: Synthesize

53
Design Template_Attitudes:
Be Mindful of Process

The Flip Stool can be flipped from an upright "perch" to a low bench.

## build instructions

The non-precious materials used to make the Flip Stool leave room for the imagination, supporting creative applications rather than forcing a particular function.

Each Flip Stool has an additional surprise: two foam cubes that pop out to be used independently.

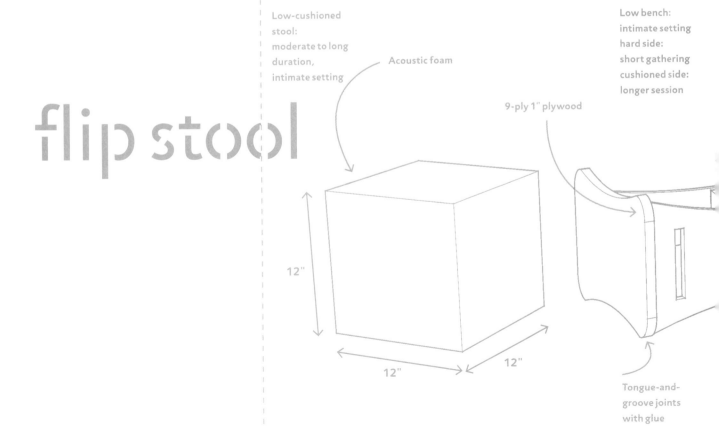

flip stool

Low-cushioned stool: moderate to long duration, intimate setting

Acoustic foam

Low bench: intimate setting hard side: short gathering cushioned side: longer session

9-ply 1" plywood

12"

12"

12"

Tongue-and-groove joints with glue

Flipping the stool is like flipping a switch between activities: the low bench provides for a comfortable reflective posture, while the tall perch supports a more actively engaged posture. These simple seats are great resources in multipurpose rooms that see a lot of use.

## start

Start simply: during your next gathering, substitute milk crates and stools for your usual seating. Keep pillows handy. Keep an eye on the ways people use each type of seat and how the uses change during the activity. Build your own Flip Stools or a variation based on what you find.

## sourcing

**manufacturing**
Rob Bell at Zomadic, LLC (San Francisco, CA; www.zomadic.com) constructed the Flip Stools. Alternatively, look for a local CNC fabricator in your neck of the woods.

**foam**
Foam Cubes (page 18) has extensive information on foam sourcing.

## see also

18
Tools_Foam Cubes

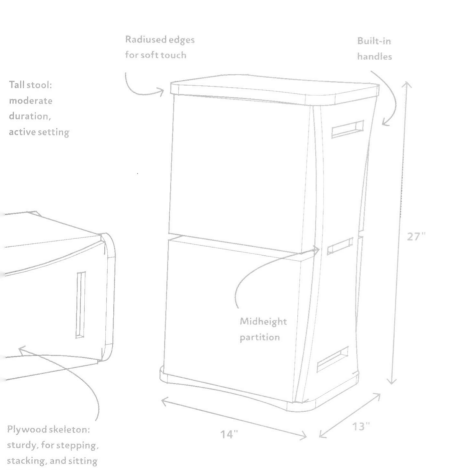

Radiused edges for soft touch

Built-in handles

Tall stool: moderate duration, active setting

27"

Midheight partition

Plywood skeleton: sturdy, for stepping, stacking, and sitting Finish: multicoat polyurethane

14"

13"

Large, uninterrupted work surfaces are literally platforms for innovation.

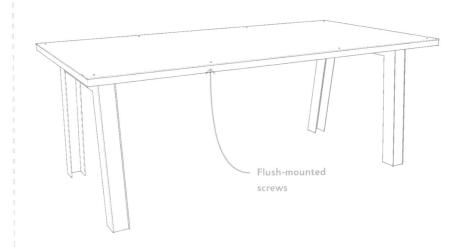

Flush-mounted screws

# prototyping tables

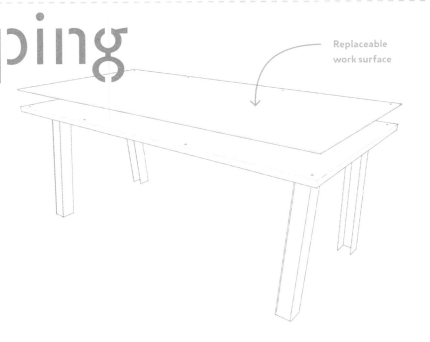

Replaceable work surface

A Prototyping Table differs from a traditional workbench in that it is clear of all tools & storage and offers accessibility from all sides. Specifically designated for project work, a Prototyping Table is an invaluable resource for exploring & embodying ideas through building.

Prototyping Tables should be big and sturdy. Make the surface as large as your space will allow. The tabletop should be thick enough to be strong & flat, but also thin enough to allow for quick clamping along the table edges. A sturdy table is often heavy—that's okay, but it is nice to be able to gang the table with another table or move it out of the way. Setting the legs in from edge of the table helps, as do heavy-duty locking casters.

An ideal work surface for light-duty prototyping is a dual-material combination: a lower plywood layer topped with a replaceable work surface.

The lower layer can be thick and heavy: try using plywood and leave the edges exposed. For the replaceable work surface, try using HDPE (high-density polyethylene) or Masonite. Secure the corners of these sheets with flush-mounting screws. When the top starts showing too much abuse from sawing, sanding, and gluing, unscrew it and flip it over to reveal a fresh, new surface. Use ¼"-thick material for the replaceable tops so that they remain evenly flat & durable.

## sourcing

### tables
The current d.school Prototyping Tables are custom prototypes manufactured by Steelcase. Previous versions have included assemblies from common plywood and prefabricated shop table legs.

### legs
Workbench legs are available at most home centers and hardware stores. McMaster-Carr (600 North County Line Road, Elmhurst, IL 60126; 630 600-3600; www.mcmaster.com) carries many varieties.

### polycarbonate/acrylic
Port Plastics (550 East Trimble Road, San Jose, CA 95131; 408 571-2231; www.portplastics.com) ships regionally.
TAP Plastics (154 South Van Ness, San Francisco, CA 94103; 800 246-5055; www.tapplastics.com) has many western U.S. locations.

### masonite
Get dual-sided, smooth Masonite. Home centers and local lumberyards keep this material in stock.

## start

Attach a 4' x 8' sheet of plywood to some prefabricated workbench legs or adjustable sawhorse legs. Obtain some Masonite or use a few fabric cutting mats for the initial tabletop surface. Place the table where it is accessible.

## see also

# Separate Idea Generation from Selection.

**Squash an idea under the weight of reality too early and you risk missing out on some valuable insights.**

Defer judgment. This gem from advertising executive Alex F. Osborn was plucked from his rules for brainstorming. It has been passed down through generations of designers and admen as a reminder to let any and all ideas flow in an effort to get to a truly excellent solution later.*

This tenet can be translated beyond brainstorming: allow creative ideas to flourish before putting them to the test. This leaves room to explore territory beyond the safe and obvious and can lead to insights that will pay off later. Don't worry—amid the realities of physics, cost, and time constraints, you'll have plenty of opportunity for pragmatism.

As an example, the idea for the d.school's Whiteboard Sliders on rails emerged from a desire to be able to instantaneously materialize a whiteboard anywhere you pleased—whiteboards could almost magically emerge as quickly as the ideas they are intended to capture. We eventually homed in on the fairly pragmatic idea of low-cost whiteboard material deployed along truss-mounted rails. However, we might have missed the opportunity had we not let ourselves entertain a seemingly ridiculous notion early on.

* Alex F. Osborn, Applied Imagination: Principles and Procedures of Creative Problem-Solving (Scribner, 1979; originally published in 1953).

## see also

**20**
Situations_Instant / Shared Studio

**58**
Tools_Whiteboard Sliders

# Don't Forget to Prototype.

**Build first. See how people react. Think about what you've learned. Repeat.**

We didn't make this up—it's a long-practiced design strategy in the public domain and has been part of Stanford's design ethos for decades. Stanford Professors Bernie Roth and Bill Burnett teach this tactic using the mantra Express, Test, Cycle. In other words, build (express); observe how people react and think about changes (test); do it again (cycle).

David Kelley, co-founder of the d.school, calls prototyping, "enlightened trial and error." In essence, the goal is to use iterative cycles of building, testing, and reflecting to make decisions and progress. The key value is using the act of building and experiential testing to illuminate insights that might never surface by thought alone.

We don't mean to suggest that research, expertise, and logical reasoning aren't worthwhile ways to tackle a problem. Use prototyping when you need to learn quickly, when you find yourself getting hung up, and when you are working on a project that has a lot of moving parts—in other words, most of the time.

Note: The foremost value of a prototype is the learning that it results in. A "failed," or poorly received, prototype that yields big insights can be far more valuable than a "successful" one that confirms previous thinking.

Work quick & dirty. It is better to answer early questions with cardboard rather than steel, in 10 minutes rather than 10 days. Plus, early ideas often have lots of gaps—you don't want them to stick around for too long. Make them rough enough so your budget and your ego won't be afraid to let them go.

## see also

53
Design Template_Attitudes: Prototype toward a Solution

108
Tools_Full-Scale Space Prototyping Toolkit

114
Insights_Work Big Early

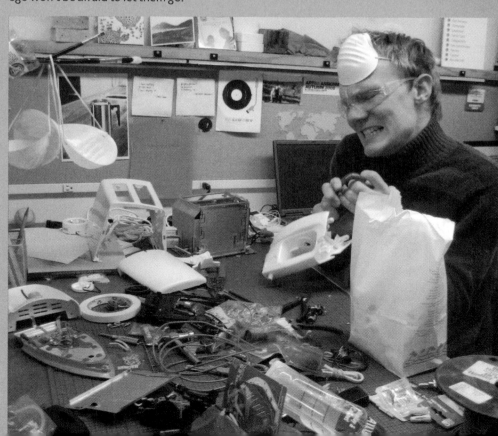

# concept car

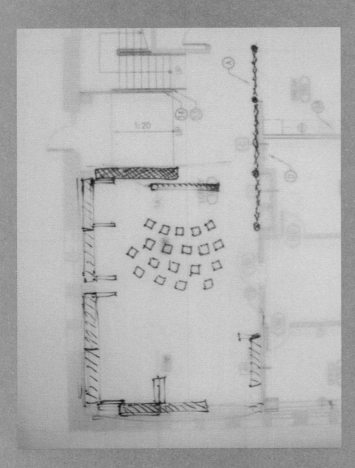

**Sketch exploring one of many activity configurations in the Concept Car.**

**Carve out part of your space to test new ideas & spatial configurations, then deploy them at scale elsewhere.** The Concept Car is a permanent place to "start small," experiment with space, and get radical at low cost. When something succeeds, deploy it elsewhere.

**Use it.**
Run workshops and meetings in the space—that's how you know if your new ideas have potential and that's how you'll get people excited about working in a dynamic environment.

**Place it in a prominent location.**
Keeping experimentation visible is a strong cultural signal.

**Turn it over frequently.**
Make it easy to reconfigure at a moment's notice and set a schedule to make regular wholesale changes.

**Provide some rigging infrastructure to make it easy to alter.**
A lighting grid of removable, adjustable gallery-style spotlights allows you to highlight different areas of the space. A Unistrut (or other pipe) grid in the ceiling provides rigging for hanging things—this works well for securing temporary "walls" and for playing with different configurations. Plywood floors allow you to drill into the floor as needed.

The Concept Car is immediately adjacent to the d.school lobby, ready for action.

## start

The Concept Car is a great starting point in itself, as soon as you have a place to start. Take over anything you can, start experimenting, and bring people in to use it.

### see also

47
Design Template_Actions

230
Tools_Grid System

Central Park in Manhattan is a designated space for continual retreat, inspiration, and expression, as evidenced by the orange-colored installation, The Gates, in 2005 by Christo and Jeanne-Claude.

# Leave Room to Evolve.

**As a new space gets used, new needs emerge. Leave room to adapt.**

**Creative people regularly generate surprising ideas and unanticipated artifacts.**
We've had a 9'-tall grain thresher and full-scale latrine prototypes appear in our space overnight. This kind of emergent work requires a different approach to work space design. The space needs to morph to support, organize, and display these unpredictable creations.

**Allow the space and the people to continue to adapt and grow.**
Do less. Leave some aspects of the space open-ended, even though your impulse might be to take care of every detail. Resist filling every square foot with furniture or decoration—literally leave room for improvement. Open space provides a buffer for identifying, absorbing, and responding to unanticipated needs. Use modular and movable infrastructure early on, so that physical change is easy. Preserve your resources in anticipation of changes down the road.

## see also

# Reimagining Space with Rapid Fabrication

## by Jeffrey McGrew and Jillian Northrup

Jeffrey "feeds" Frank, the CNC router, with commands and materials.

**Frank**

We discovered digital fabrication using computerized numerical control (CNC) tools about five years ago. Since then, we've been working to perfect the process for our small design studio, Because We Can. While both of us enjoy physically making things in our personal time, neither of us comes from a professional hands-on crafting background. Our careers were in creative fields that leaned heavily on computer-aided work (Jeffrey being an architect, and Jillian a designer and photographer). We now incorporate all of that in real time by transforming three-dimensional digital models into physical assemblies, using our in-house CNC shop.

Our main machine is a 5-foot by 10-foot three-axis CNC router we call Frank. Most everything we design gets sliced into parts and sections and fed to him. Anything we can model in 3-D, we can quickly make real in a mostly automated way. Small-scale digital fabrication empowers us to make the world a more interesting place through the creation of novel artifacts. In our last warehouse space we made 12-foot by 12-foot doors with smaller 8-foot by 8-foot doors inside of them. And it was no big deal!

**Rapid retooling of the Library Lounge**
When we moved into our new facility in Oakland, it contained an odd nook of a room on the first floor with no outside facing windows and no door to enclose it from a busy hallway. Its location and size made it awkward to use—we stored our bikes in it for a while—but it never felt properly utilized. We decided to make this a hang-out space where we could get away from the upstairs office, find inspiration, meet, and reflect. We envisioned a place where we could sit and flip through the many design books we have collected over the years. A library was just the thing.

**Use what we have and build
what we need**
In planning the library, we looked first at what we had left over from our previous location: a large, shallow rolling hutch and a long midcentury couch from a former bus station. Using these bits as a starting point, we tipped our hats to the midcentury modern aesthetic when designing the new bookcases and seating we'd need.

Because our workflow allows us to move fluidly from digital designs to fabrication, we were revising the 3-D models in our spare time on Wednesday and cutting out our bookshelves

by Friday. We assembled them that Saturday, and on Sunday we picked out the fabric for the cushions. After finishing the first shelves, we were inspired to do something with more color and decided on a playful paint job.

**Tuning the details**
Realizing this small space needed to be used very efficiently, we designed the shelves to incorporate additional seating. Because we rent the space, we made everything freestanding, so it can come with us when we move. Art and assorted knickknacks found themselves among the books. We switched out lighting fixtures, and the addition of a striking carpet completed the transformation from a bare, concrete-floored space into a cozy nook—designed to inspire.

**Imagination begets fabrication,
fabrication begets imagination**
Because we are directly involved in the fabrication process of our designs, we have the opportunity to be inspired by the fabrication process and allow it to directly influence the overall creation process. With the speed of digital fabrication, it's easy to make changes or new parts embodying fresh ideas. We find that the final touches and the

special details make single pieces and entire spaces shine. Frank's agility and our willingness to experiment with him creates more opportunities for these details, whether they are aesthetic touches like the upholstered seating on bookshelves or assembly sequences that make pieces easier to install. His proximity gives us a chance to respond to chance happenings and random ideas, his speed allows us to test our assumptions physically, and his programmable nature lets us iterate at the drop of a hat. This agility empowers us to make substantial changes to the physical environment; we take far more creative risks than we would without him.

Jeffrey McGrew and Jillian Northrup are designers and builders. They own and operate Because We Can, a design studio in Oakland, California. Their work ranges from one-of-a-kind installations to commercially available consumer products.

The library nook revamp in progress: before, during, and after.

Create custom furniture
and parts—cheaply
and quickly—with basic
graphic files and a local
fabricator.

Rob Bell, of
Zomadic,
LLC, cutting &
assembling the
d.school Scoop
Stools.

# local
# fabrication
# shop

Fabrication machinery is now in a state of reliability such that small manufacturers can work from simple digital graphic files that you can generate using readily available software: Google SketchUp (free!) and Adobe Illustrator are examples. Most graphics generated from these files can be saved as or converted to a .dxf file. This type of file easily incorporates with control software for most equipment.

Plotter printers, laser-cutting equipment, and CNC routers can all pro-duce large-scale components you can use to create bold environments. When the base materials consist of plywood, Masonite, or rigid foamboard, fabrica-tion costs can be low and production times can be hours or days, not weeks.

The d.school has created much of its furniture using these techniques: the Bleacher Blocks, Flip Stools, Aesthetic Panels, and the Lanterns are some examples. The implementations are seemingly endless: stools, tables, desks, panels, tools, building blocks . . . there are all sorts of possibilities for you to quickly construct an environment that is uniquely suited to your purpose. In many cases, these techniques are cheap and quick enough to use for both prototypes and the finished products.

## sourcing

Local manufacturers are accessible, and they are often networked, with particular businesses focusing on a particular piece of machinery or operation. The d.school has developed strong relationships with many shops in the San Francisco Bay Area; each of these shops has also led to further connections.

Zomadic, LLC (San Francisco, CA; www.zomadic.com)

Because We Can (2500 Kirkham Street, Oakland, CA 94607; 510 922-8846; www.becausewecan.org)

Monkey Wrench Designs (1234 Folsom Street, San Francisco, CA 94103; www.mwdes.com)

## start

Download Google SketchUp. Give yourself a couple of hours to learn how to use it (the how-tos are excellent!). Draw a shape. Save that file as a .dxf and find a shop to work with you to cut it from the material you select. To get started, look for shops offering CNC services, millwork & routing services, and laser-cutting services.

## see also

68
Tools_Flip Stool

138
Tools_Lanterns

152
Tools_Aesthetic Panels

180
Tools_Bleacher Blocks

Create 360-degree engagement with dual-surface projection.

Concrete anchors

Rigid frame won't "sag"

Threaded steel rod

hanging screen

Slotted wood frame (like a stretcher for a painting canvas)

Frosted reflection surface bounces light off the front and lets light pass through the back.

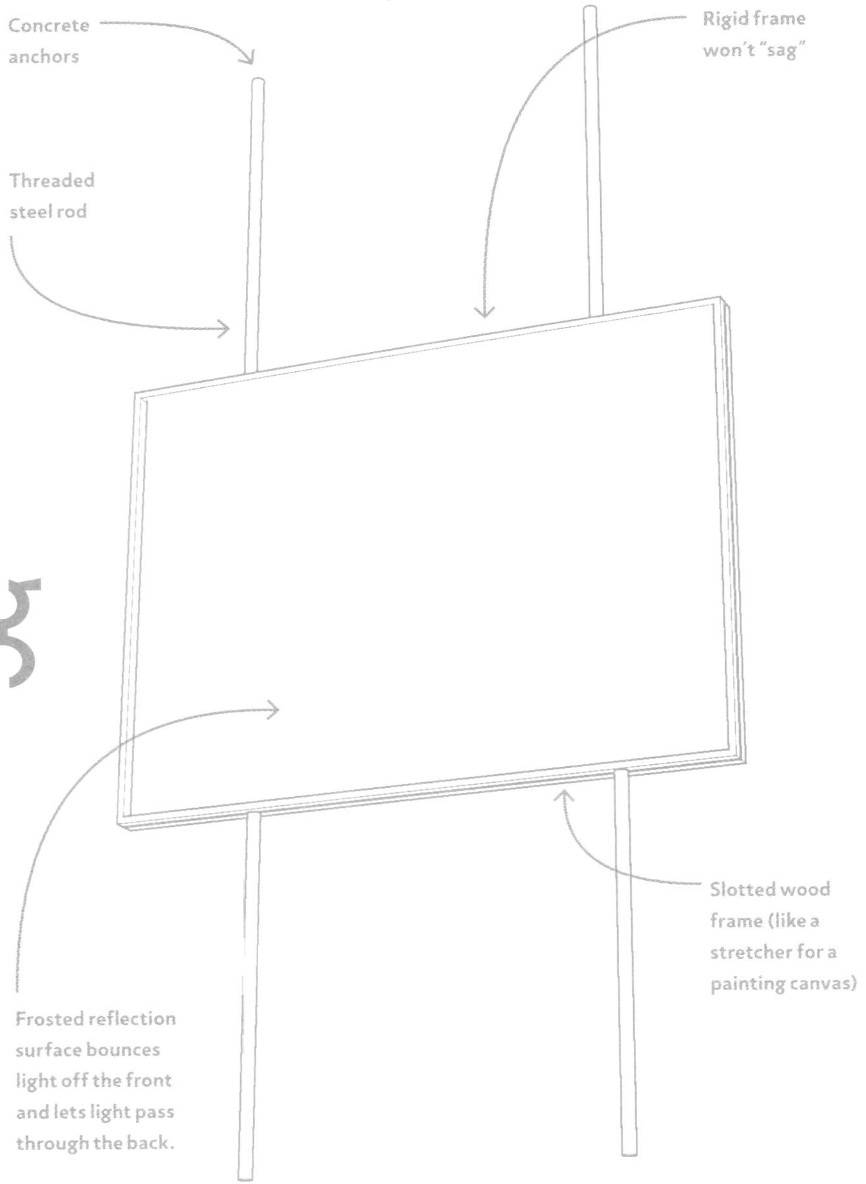

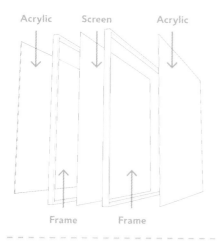

Acrylic sheet sandwich with frosted
projection screen material in the middle

Acrylic — Screen — Acrylic

Frame — Frame

Use a "short-throw" projector
with a bright image (3000+ lumens)

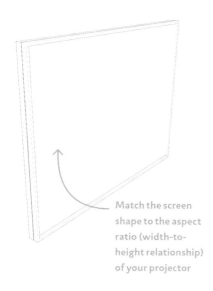

Match the screen
shape to the aspect
ratio (width-to-
height relationship)
of your projector

The hanging screen displays images
on its front and back surfaces as an
effect of the semitransparent screen
construction. This two-sided image
takes bystanders by surprise with a view
of the action. The backside projection
is reversed (words are not completely
legible), but the vibe of the activity is
clear & the image signals that the room
is in use.

### Choosing a Projector
Get a short-throw projector: it can
create a big image (4' tall) from a short
screen distance (as close as 3') and will
eliminate shadows as people approach
the screen—and they will.

Match the screen shape to the
aspect ratio (width-to-height relationship) of your projector. Projectors often
come in 4:3 or 16:9 (widescreen)—it's
your call on which to use. The scale of
the image is dictated by the projector
position. Test projector placement to
confirm the size and shape of the screen
you'll need.

### Hanging the screen
Mount the edges of the frame to the
ceiling/overhead structure. Keep the
screen from swinging by stabilizing it
from the floor, a nearby wall, or another
installation. Example: We installed a
screen into overhead concrete using
anchors and threaded rod; the screen is
stabilized by a connection to a low counter beneath the installation location.

## start

Test the concept by projecting onto
a sheet of frosted Mylar suspended
from the ceiling. See how it works
before moving on to something
more permanent.

## sourcing

**manufacturing**
Because We Can (2500 Kirkham Street,
Oakland, CA 94607; 510 922-8846;
www.becausewecan.org) manufactured the
d.school's Hanging Screen.

**acrylic**
Port Plastics (550 East Trimble Road, San Jose, CA
95131; 408 571-2231; www.portplastics.com)
ships regionally.
TAP Plastics (154 South Van Ness, San Francisco,
CA 94103; 800 246-5055; www.tapplastics
.com) has many western U.S. locations.

**screen material**
Da-Lite Dual Vision Screen Material
(www.da-lite.com)

## see also

140
Tools_HACK: Frosted Polyester Film
Mini-Screens

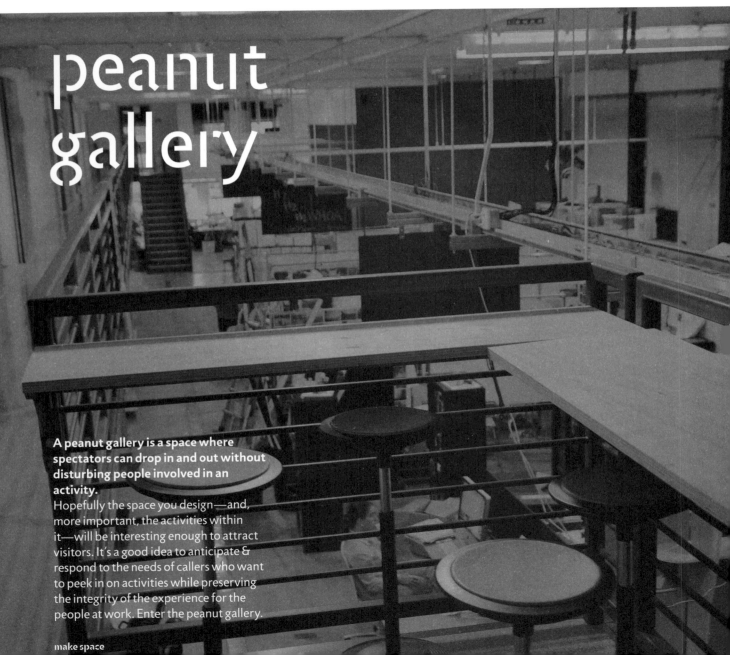

# peanut gallery

**A peanut gallery is a space where spectators can drop in and out without disturbing people involved in an activity.**
Hopefully the space you design—and, more important, the activities within it—will be interesting enough to attract visitors. It's a good idea to anticipate & respond to the needs of callers who want to peek in on activities while preserving the integrity of the experience for the people at work. Enter the peanut gallery.

**start**

Depending on available space, additional tables and partitions may not work. Try keeping several tall stools along a wall adjacent to a high-visibility work area or in a transition space, preferably near a back entrance. Monitor the way spectators engage.

**see also**

121
Insights_Use Soft Boundaries to Partition Open Spaces

**A useful peanut gallery . . .**

**Provides a strong visual delineation that can be broken on occasion.**
A railing or long bar-style surface is terrific for this. It provides a strong line that separates spectators from participants but still allows for discussion if the spectators are engaged. A glass wall provides a more solid delineation but is more difficult to violate.

**Allows people to come and go quietly.**
For this reason, tall stools are useful, as they allow someone to move from standing to sitting and back to standing with little commotion.

# Make a Soundtrack.

A great leader is a good host. A good host sets the tone for guests. Music can help curate experiences in the classroom, design studio, office . . . anywhere.

**Intent trumps style—almost any genre can work.**
The trick is to avoid a distracting ambience. We bias toward a lively but relaxed and reflective mood when students arrive, and something upbeat for when they leave.

Sure, music acts on the emotions, but our (unsubstantiated) hypothesis is that during active work (such as proto-typing) music also occupies just enough of our cognitive load to distract our inner critic. As long as it's upbeat, music seems to propel creative activities, but there are some subtleties to consider.

## Volume
It seems fine to raise the volume above background level: some bopping, danc-ing, and whistling are good indicators that the music is working. That said, music that is too loud can be distracting, although this is a judgment call. Can you hear a side comment from your neighbor? If so, the music is either too quiet or just right. If not, the music is too loud.

## Lyrics
As a rule of thumb, avoid lyrics—they're distracting. Occasionally a song that has prominent lyrics still works for reasons unknown: Beck's "Que Onda Guero" seems to be such a track.

## Repetition & Rhythm
Repetitive music with a prominent rhythm keeps people focused on the task at hand. Lee Morgan's song "The Sidewinder" is a good example.

## Tone & Familiarity
Music can add urgency or calm the nerves. Something to consider: do you use music that is familiar to all or something that is a bit exotic? Go with your gut, be intentional, and don't overdo it—you'll know.

# Build in Little Rituals.

**Deliberately incorporating a ritual into a routine can transform the mundane into a minor magic moment.**

Take off your shoes before you walk into this room. What? Why! My feet smell and my socks have holes. Already, the moment has been transformed, and the mental baggage of beginning a meeting has been unloaded.

## see also

The Google office in Zurich, Switzerland. Design by Camendzin Evolution Ltd.

# Special Touches Create a Sense of Belonging.

**"Owned" space signals that an individual has standing in the community. In a shared, open, and collaborative environment, you need to find novel ways to provide people with feelings of ownership.**

**Once folks get settled in, you might be the target of a bit of angst.**
You're experiencing nothing less than the deep-seated fear of mortality. Really. When we work with less and give up the spatial signifiers of our existence (offices, signage, etc.), we start to feel a little more vulnerable. This feeling begins at around age two, when we're forced to share our toys, and it never goes away. This vulnerability can manifest itself as a lost sense of belonging.

**When a space feels extra-special, it has a cascading impact.**
Beyond the fact that it's simply an enjoyable place to be, people like to show it off and share it with family and friends. They get positive feedback from this, and that vibe fuels a feeling of pride; with pride comes a feeling of ownership; with ownership comes a sense of belonging. Voila!

**What constitutes a special touch?**
Think in terms of materials, ambience, and surprises.

**Unique & remarkable materials:**
As an example, the d.school has a mesquite end-grain parquet floor in the full-time staff suite. It's unique, the color is lovely and natural, the style is timeless, it contrasts with the adjacent concrete floor, and it wears well (a must for the way we beat up our spaces).

**Analog ambience:**
Custom carpets. Windows that open to the outside. Incandescent lights. Music. All these things make a space more livable.

**Surprises:**
Anything that violates a norm in a playful way. Peter McGraw, of the Humor Research Lab (HURL) at the University of Colorado at Boulder, describes humor as a "benign violation."* Where can you insert a benign violation? The d.school has turned bathrooms into faux forests and dance halls. Google has installed the occasional slide in place of a staircase. The Pixar staff uses its atrium space as a dodgeball court . . . okay, sometimes it isn't so benign.

*Peter McGraw and Caleb Warren, "Benign violations: Making immoral behavior funny," Psychological Science, 2010.

see also

45
Design Template_Properties: Ambience

115
Insights_Use Space to Level Status

116
Insights_Space Is Not Always the Solution

196
Insights_The Open Office Floor Plan Has a Shadow

A properly designed
sign is mighty fine.

# signs
# that
# POP

extreme
studio

workspaces and materials
are owned by student teams

524A

c-space

Vinyl lettering
on acrylic or
polycarbonate
looks pro.

Black text on a
white background
creates compelling
contrast.

A special shape
can convey
importance: this
subtle cue makes
a difference in
amplifying your
message.

Consider scale:
when in doubt,
make your
signs bigger.

Spray-adhering
paper to foamboard
is quick & easy,
and it looks great.

Make your signs
consistent: use the
same font & tone of
voice for all of them.

Leave white
space to make
messages pop.

Create signs that communicate clearly and convey the vibe & emotion of your environment. Make them easy to modify—as usage changes, so should your signs.

Meaningful messaging includes crisp, intentional language and clear & compelling visual delivery. Make your messages short, with unambiguous directions: "Clean this room." Use the same font & tone of voice throughout to make your signage consistent.

Craft the details of your signs. Spending an extra second (literally) to go one step beyond an 8 1/2" x 11" sheet of paper taped on a window communicates intentionality.

Hide your attachments or make them scream: every detail communicates a message. Try using Velcro or painter's tape on the back of a sign to make it easy to reposition and/or reconfigure. Install grommets to mount signs on hooks: the appeal of a "shingle" sign is its shock value.

## start

Make some square signs. For each, create a text file and print a concise message on a sheet of 8 1/2" x 11" paper. Center the text in an 8 1/2" x 8 1/2" square on the page and leave wide margins all around. Spray-adhere the paper to a piece of foamboard. Trim the long dimension down to 8 1/2" and install your sign.

### see also

**94**
Tools_Vinyl Cutter

**150**
Tools_Bulk Sheet Materials

Buy a vinyl cutter.
Do it now.

Use vinyl for distinctive wayfinding signage (top), instructional labeling of tools (middle), and decoration/branding (bottom).

vinyl
cutter

This is a transformative step in the process of creating & controlling the look and feel of your space. Creating signs and graphics is far more significant than making simple labels—it is a major move toward communicating your culture and sharing your brand. This is an excellent step for start-ups as well as groups within major organizations.

Believe it on not, buying a vinyl cutter will save you money. It pays for itself quickly when compared to outsourcing even a single midsized graphics project. The immediate accessibility and manipulability afforded by the vinyl cutter encourage new & inventive applications that would otherwise be prohibitive due to time and cost.

Generating adhesive graphics is a simple printing-and-cutting process. It does take a little bit of time to become thoroughly familiar with the process of generating a digital file, cutting the adhesive vinyl, and applying the sticker to surfaces. The result is worth it: being able to quickly & confidently embellish the visual landscape with graphics, serious or whimsical, is a critical characteristic in a communicative culture. This approach can transform the function of communication from mere warning signs and labeling (prescriptive) to curated experiences (participatory). The fit and finish of the vinyl messaging makes the space feel intentional & unique.

## tips

· Practice positioning and applying the adhesive layer a few times on sample graphics until you become comfortable. This is easy to do, but it requires patience.
· As you place the graphics, it can be helpful to use a plastic putty knife or spatula to press the graphics firmly in place on the desired surface before finally peeling away the adhesive sheet.

## sourcing

**cutter**
The Roland CAMM-1 Servo GX-24 vinyl cutter is a superior performer. It handles a wide variety of sheet materials, finishes, and sizes.
Roland DGA (www.rolanddga.com)

**vinyl**
Many colors, thicknesses, and widths of bulk vinyl materials are available.
Product Sign Supplies (625 Emory Street, San Jose, CA 95110; 800 540-9199; www.productsignsupplies.com)

## start

Make your coffeemaker sing: how do you make coffee in a commercial-style machine? It can be confusing! While a standard approach might be to post a conventional sign above the machine, a more intimate & fun approach is to apply custom-prepared vinyl graphics & text directly to the equipment.

Vinyl graphics are surprisingly useful for creating subtle messaging throughout an environment. Try adding some cartoon or graphical elements in hallways or around high-traffic areas.

## see also

92
Tools_Signs That POP

# Make Technology Radically Accessible, But Don't Use It Often.

**Keep the latest technology around and available, but learn when to use it and when not to.**

Digital technology is now and forever an indispensable part of the creative process.

Radically accessible tools inspire experiments and minimize time spent searching for the "right" resources. But beware when technology becomes a focus in itself.

When the technology has been purchased and made available, we're inclined to use it, regardless of whether it is a good idea or not. Consider this cultural phenomenon: in the 1990s, the rash of car chases televised by local news helicopters seemed to correspond with the purchase of helicopters by local news stations. Hmmm, we just bought a helicopter, what should we do with it?

Laptops, smart phones, and computer tablets are revolutionary tools, but listen to a room full of people meeting while simultaneously focusing on their laptop screens and you'll hear the staccato rhythms of distracted conversations. Never mind the content displayed on the screen, the physical laptop screen itself erects its own little wall of separation between people, who automatically sequester themselves in the hunched posture they assumed while taking standardized tests in high school.

## see also

159
Insights_Beware of Whiz-Bang!

185
Insights_Technology in Your Pocket

# Pick Your Spending Spots.

**Spend money where it matters (and don't where it doesn't).**
Before designing a new environment, note spaces likely to have the most impact and prioritize the spending for those spots. As budgets are often tight, this will require you to spend money unevenly across your project. Spend less in places where you can get away with it so you can spend more where it really matters. Where does it matter? This depends on the nature of your space, but there are some common possibilities.

**Thresholds, active areas, and elsewhere.**
Thresholds: They set the tone for the rest of the experience.

High-use areas: Places that people use a lot should feel good throughout the whole experience—entrance, activity, and exit.

Surprise spots: A detail deep within the building can create a sense of surprise that permeates the space. If there is a space that you wish people would occupy (e.g., a gathering space), make it special.

see also

40
Design Template_Places

90
Insights_Special Touches Create a Sense of Belonging

179
Insights_Don't Blow the Whole Budget

# cul-de-sac

**The metaphorical cul-de-sac is a spot at which to linger and chat before or after a gathering.**
Aim to create a comfortable pause zone, where conversations can transpire that might otherwise have been lost.

**People love to strike up conversations at thresholds, on their way in and out of spaces.**
These transitions are sometimes the only moments people have to catch up. In his epic dissection of space, Social Life of Small Urban Spaces —a must-see!— William H. Whyte calls these chats, "impromptu conferences" or "protracted good-byes." (He also notes that these conversations often take place in the middle of traffic flows.)

**Our most successful cul-de-sacs are simply the arms and backs of couches.**
We often have couches in the classroom, and these become cul-de-sacs for conversations as people rest a knee on the arm or lean against the back of the couch.

**In a nutshell, a successful cul-de-sac is an open space in or near the flow of traffic combined with an object of attraction that can be engaged & released with little or no effort.**

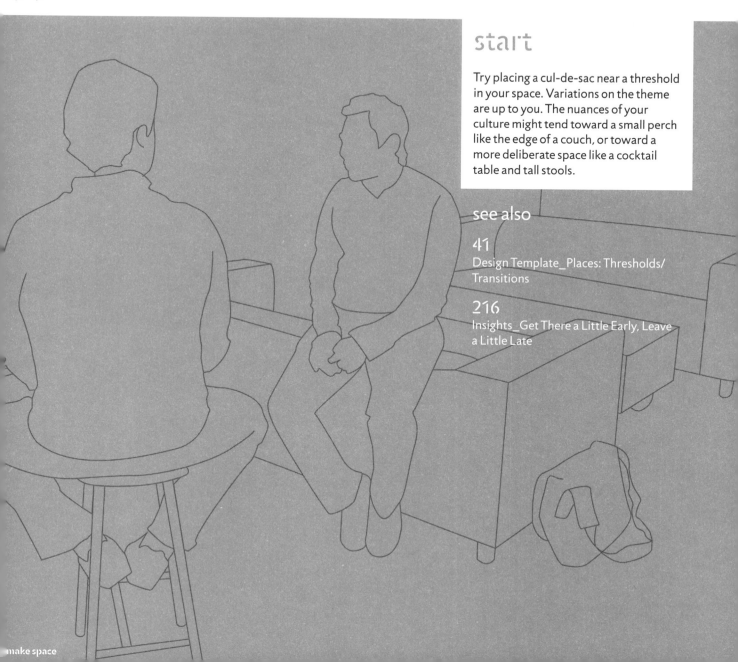

## start

Try placing a cul-de-sac near a threshold in your space. Variations on the theme are up to you. The nuances of your culture might tend toward a small perch like the edge of a couch, or toward a more deliberate space like a cocktail table and tall stools.

## see also

### 41
Design Template_Places: Thresholds/ Transitions

### 216
Insights_Get There a Little Early, Leave a Little Late

# anchors

**The more flexible a space is, the more some things need to stay fixed.**

**It is especially important to keep community tools (copiers, shared computers) and amenities (food, supplies) in prominent and fixed locations.**

Anchors build "muscle memory" within the organization and offer extended members of the community an easier engagement: though work spaces may change daily, everyone always knows where the food and the copier are. This ability to dive right in despite any changes in the surroundings is good for efficiency (no hand-holding necessary) and a personal sense of belonging (feeling at home).

**In a home base.**
Keep the coffee and food available and the copiers and printers well maintained. People will be happier.

**In a gathering space.**
It's fine to let the furniture migrate, but keep materials and tools (phones, projectors) in fixed or at least highly visible locations.

The San Francisco office space for Timbuk2 prior to move-in.

**An example:**
For a collaborative work space at the messenger bag company Timbuk2, Architect John Lum had one of the 15' columns painted. It stood like a totem in the middle of the otherwise white-walled space, deep orange as a way to advertise the location of the copy area.

## start

This is easy: it's what not to do. Make a list of items (such as the copiers) that should remain fixed. Don't move them. Use bright paint and/or prominent signage to signal their presence in the space.

## see also

40
Design Template_Places

134
Insights_Design Strong Points & Counterpoints

# Enter on Action.

**Have visitors enter an active (rather than empty) space to give them an immediate feel for the culture of a place.**

Screenwriters tout the benefits of starting a script or scene in media res, or "in the middle of things." This pulls the audience into the story by placing the action up front. The same principle can be applied to space.

Welcome areas that are easy to navigate are critical for helping visitors feel at home in a space. Equally important is getting guests excited by the buzz and vibe of a community. Sometimes losing a wall or adding some glass between an entry zone and an active area is all it takes.

**One caveat: Don't overdo it.** Transitions are important. Let guests feel the energy of the space immediately, but allow them to enter it on their terms by offering a visible threshold between themselves and the action—through floor treatment, a glass wall, or a partial partition.

## see also

41
Design Template_Places: Transitions / Thresholds

97
Insights_Pick Your Spending Spots

# Provide Room to Think.

**"The point about working is not to produce great stuff all the time, but to remain ready for when you can." —Brian Eno***

**Anecdotes abound of insights arriving in strange places.**
Two professors we know (one at Stanford, one at UCLA) describe the need to travel or experience a change of scene to work out an idea. Digital artist and creator of the We Feel Fine website Jonathan Harris† explains that "[ideas] aggregate over time then pop out one day when you are in the shower."‡ As Jonah Lehrer explains, these anecdotes are beginning to find support from brain research as EEG studies of the brain show that insights, ideas, and epiphanies occur when the brain is most relaxed. §

**Creating nonwork places at work is actually productive in a creative environment.**
Encourage relaxation amid a stressful and strained work environment by providing spaces for quiet reflection and temporary escape. Outfit these spaces with appointments and surfaces—pillows, wallpaper, etc.—that grant permission not to work.

* Eric Tamm, Brian Eno: His Music and the Vertical Sound of Color (Da Capo, 1995); † Jonathan Harris and Sep Kamvar, www.wefeelfine.org; ‡Scott Belsky, Making Ideas Happen (Portfolio, 2010); §Jonah Lehrer, "The Eureka Hunt," The New Yorker, July 28, 2008.

see also

132
Situations_Hiding Place

Interior of James Turrell's installation, Three Gems, at the DeYoung Museum, San Francisco.

# The d.school Sandbox

## by Scott Doorley and Scott Witthoft

make space

Design Thinking Bootcamp is a class at the d.school that introduces students to design through project-based learning. The class requires intimate spaces for teams of students to work on their projects. In Fall 2007, we created a variety of spaces for the class to explore how teams' working environments affect collaboration and the quality of their designs.

In our observation of team-based collaborations among d.school students, we had noticed that there seemed to be a correlation between students' posture and their ability to generate ideas. For example, students comfortably seated on couches often settled back into criticizing others' ideas rather than jumping into creating new ones. We decided to test the validity of this observation by creating four prototypes, each designed to inspire students to assume postures we wanted to investigate—from low and relaxed to upright and active.

To promote an upright seating posture, we clustered students in straight-backed chairs around a table and dubbed that situation the "War Room." In another situation, we gave students the opportunity to lean back on soft couches, in a faux "Lounge" foot-print. One extreme configuration, the "Dance Floor," consisted of a bounded area of floor space that, flanked by swings and devoid of any other seating options, encouraged students to stand and move around.

"war room"

"dance floor"

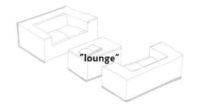
"lounge"

"sandbox"

left: Students with a teaching assistant, crouching and reclining in the sandbox prototype.

above: The four prototypes designed to elicit variations in students' postures.

# Space Studies_The d.school Sandbox

The fourth counterpoint configuration was the "Sandbox," a wooden box placed on the floor with a padded interior for seating. We hypothesized that the playfulness of the space combined with the extreme posture that students had to assume while sitting on the floor would encourage them to relax and lower their barriers to interacting with one another.

The most compelling things we learned came from observing students in the class while they used the more extreme designs. For instance, as a functional team space, the Sandbox was an absolute disaster. The collective response was precisely the opposite of what we had intended: although the floor seating was soft and comfortable, the students, in fact, did not feel comfortable. Sitting close to one another—as dictated by the boundaries created by the edges of the space—made for a forced intimacy. The low seating made it difficult for students to get up, slowing the exchange of leadership. When students did rise, they loomed over team members like Godzilla over Tokyo. Contrarily, the upright and active postures of students on the Dance Floor facilitated a hearty crop of ideas. Energy within groups using that space was high, with lively interplay among the students.

The success from the Sandbox's failure to produce a space that enhanced collaboration was a shining example that posture does indeed

have a profound effect on students' behavior. Building on the nugget of posture extremes and how it influences idea generation, our latest exploits have been pairing props (such as bar stools) and environments (such as wide-open spaces) to encourage upright and active postures. Through simple prototyping with postures as a focus, we found that even the slightest attention toward posture—standing versus sitting—for example, can greatly amplify the potential of design collaborations.

Scott Doorley is Creative Director and Co-Director of the Environments Collaborative at the Stanford University d.school. He was a d.school Fellow from 2006 to 2007.

Scott Witthoft is Co-Director of the Environments Collaborative at the Stanford University d.school. He was a d.school Fellow from 2008 to 2009.

Current configuration
for teams, promoting
energetic posture.

Prototyping a space at full scale is a critical step early in the design of your space.

full-scale space prototyping toolkit

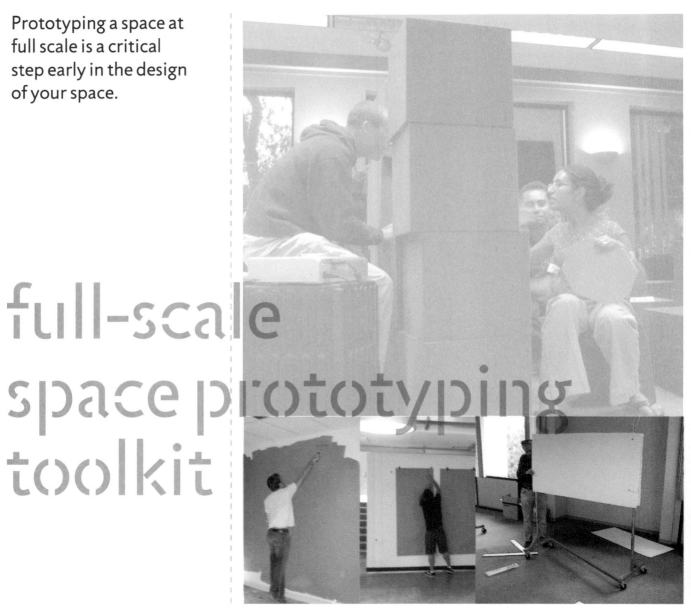

Full-scale prototyping is advantageous in the long run because it accelerates conversations among all parties: facilities planners, architects, engineers, your people, and you. Call it whatever you like in order to get started: mock-up, prototype, or exploration. It can help you work out design challenges, recognize new opportunities, get acquainted with the physicality & feeling of a space, and get your community excited about the possibilities.

**bare minimum kit: $50–$100**
**your imagination, plus:**
· butcher paper
· packing boxes
· matte knife & scissors
· measuring tape
· blue painter's tape
· packing tape
· bright-colored twine
· chalk

**deluxe kit, $500 and up**
**same items as the bare minimum kit, plus:**
· Foam Cubes (quantity: 20+)
· 4' x 8' foamboard (quantity: 20+)
· sawhorses (quantity: 10+)
· lumber: 2x2s in 12' lengths (quantity: 20)
· wood screws: 3" length
· saw (circular or a handsaw)
· clamps
· sample furniture on casters
· furniture dollies
· Z-Racks
· carpet squares

## tips

· Make wall corners out of the foamboard to emulate room boundaries.
· Use the sawhorses to keep the foamboard upright. These create nice movable walls.
· Furniture dollies are great for moving existing nonwheeled furniture that you want to rearrange.
· Add anything you think is important. Want to explore a color? Do a quick single coat of paint on a wall—you'll be amazed at what you can accomplish with a roller in 10 minutes if you're not worried about edges or roller marks.
· Estimate the sizes of the furniture you might use. Cut 2-D models at scale from foamboard or boxes and play with them in the space.
· Advanced: Build simple frames from 2x2 lumber & screws to simulate furniture or infrastructure at scale.

## sourcing

A lot of this stuff (painter's tape, chalk, matte knives, clamps, saws, etc.) is available at your local hardware store.

**foamboard**
Foamboard & cardboard are available at art & architectural suppliers.
Arch Supplies (99 Missouri, San Francisco, CA 94107; 415 433-2724; www.archsupplies.com)
ULINE Shipping Supply Specialists (800 958-5463; www.uline.com)

**boxes**
Packing boxes are available at moving and shipping stores such as U-Haul (www.uhaul.com).

## start

Acquire access to your site at an early stage—even during construction. Just take a bunch of lightweight, big, malleable, and expendable objects to the space and start experimenting with different layouts. Be prepared: go in with a plan. What problems do you want to work out? The entry? A seating configuration? Document your actions: move objects around and take pictures and sketch the ideas on floor plans.

**paper**
Butcher paper, brown and white, in various dimensions:
Kelly Paper (1375 Howard Street, San Francisco, CA 94103; 415 522-0420; www.kellypaper.com) has many regional locations.

**carpet**
Modular carpet squares: FLOR (600 West Van Buren Street, Suite 800, Chicago, IL 60607; 866 952-4093; www.flor.com)

## see also

Shrink a project space to wall + storage space when not in use, and you get the best of both worlds: persistent project work with lots of available space for other projects & teams.

# expandable team spaces

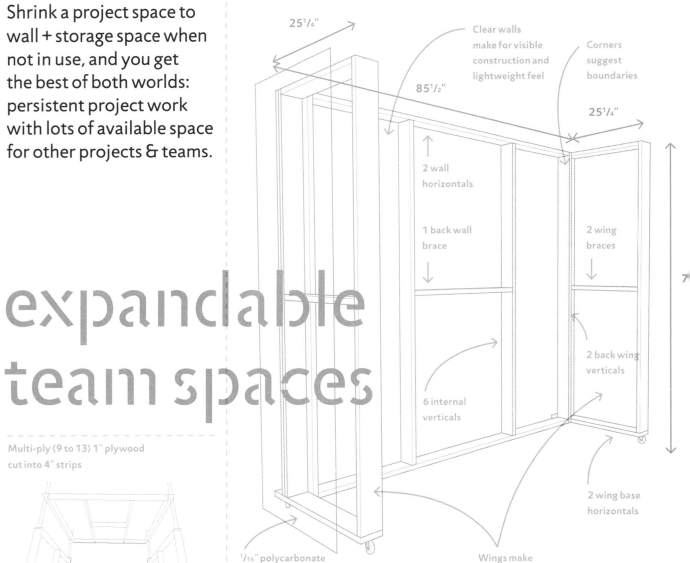

25¹/₄"

85¹/₂"

25¹/₄"

Clear walls make for visible construction and lightweight feel

Corners suggest boundaries

2 wall horizontals

1 back wall brace

2 wing braces

2 back wing verticals

6 internal verticals

2 wing base horizontals

Wings make it stable

¹/₁₆" polycarbonate sheet

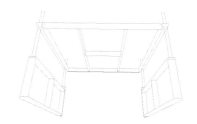

Multi-ply (9 to 13) 1" plywood cut into 4" strips

The Expandable Team Space reduces inactive project space by compacting project materials to a 3' x 6' footprint. This tightly packed space constitutes the anchor for a much larger team space when it's engaged: work in progress always stays in place, while floor space is freed up when it's not in use.

As pictured, the Team Space provides a mobile, active project wall. Add a low shelf or a Storage Tower if a team needs a workbench or more storage.

## build instructions

**Build it yourself or hire a carpenter.**

1. Cut the plywood into 4"-wide strips with a table or panel saw.

2. A less elegant but easy alternative: use 2x4s in place of the plywood strips; adjust the dimensions accordingly!

3. Frame out the main wall & the wings.

4. Attach the wings to the back wall.

5. Cut the polycarbonate to skin the walls.

6. Drill hole patterns in the polycarbonate sheets. Use wide-head screws to attach the polycarbonate to the wall frame.

7. Attach the casters.

8. Add hooks or mount a large kitchen-type drawer for additional storage.

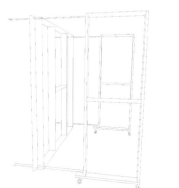

**Note:**
Countersink flat screws in wood parts.
Use wide head screws on polycarbonate / skins.
Use self-drilling screws for speed.
Nest horizontals inside the verticals.
Use 2" casters with full rotation—low & sturdy.

## sourcing

**manufacturing**
The d.school Expandable Team Spaces were constructed by Jeff Couture. (Stingray Builders Inc.; stingraybuilders.com)

**wood**
Lumber is available at local lumber and hardware stores or home centers.

**hardware**
Kitchen drawer handles are available at IKEA (www.ikea.com).

**heavy-duty casters**
Industrial Caster & Wheel Co. (2200 Carden Street, San Leandro, CA 94577; 510 569-8303; www.icwco.com)

## start

The key is to shrink project work to just wall plus storage space when teams are inactive, then place the stored project work near open floor space. This can be tried immediately by giving teams sheets of foamboard and a designated slice of a wall in a shared project suite.

California Caster and Hand Truck Company (1400 17th Street, San Francisco, CA 94107; 800 950-8750; www.californiacaster.com)

**polycarbonate sheets**
Port Plastics (550 East Trimble Road, San Jose, CA 95131; 408 571-2231; www.portplastics.com) ships regionally.
TAP Plastics (154 South Van Ness, San Francisco, CA 94103; 800 246-5055; www.tapplastics.com) has many western U.S. locations.

## see also

# studio classroom

**With some thanks to high technology, there is a good argument that a low-tech, "old school" studio-style room might be the classroom of the future.**

Technology can now deliver expert-to-student content (e.g., video talks) anytime, anywhere. The ubiquity of content opens the opportunity for the in-classroom experience to support collaboration and practice with the teacher as a guide or mentor. This flip—content outside class, work in class—is often referred to as the "reverse classroom." The studio classroom takes advantage of this opportunity; it sets the stage for maximum hands-on experimentation and for students to connect with each other in class.

**The facets of a studio classroom:**

**Patina gives permission: use non-precious materials.**
Rough materials encourage active, messy work; they signal that they don't need to be handled with care.

**Alternate between the needs of a large group and those of a small group.**
Studio classes fluctuate between lecture—collective focus on a single source—and activity—group work and intimate focus between peers. Situating students around team tables rather than in seated rows allows these switches to occur quickly, as do rolling partitions like the Z-Racks.

**Design for transitions.**
As the class activities fluctuate, the space will likely need to be reconfigured. Lightweight furniture and furniture with wheels make transitions easy.

**Use limits to inspire creativity.**
Fewer choices are much easier to approach and manipulate. For instance, we use rail-mounted Whiteboard Sliders that limit choice to only two options: deploy or store. Teaching teams can create several situations with this simple choice: treat them as room scale dividers or use them to define individual team spaces.

**Set aside "before" and "after" time.**
Professors and students love to engage before class and linger afterward, and an active studio requires time for breakdown and setup. Schedule use of the room to provide for a healthy amount of time before and after class. We reserve 45 minutes between classes.

# Work Big Early.

**Work at full-scale first.**

From a typical planning point of view, this seems backward, since projects often begin with planning and feasibility studies and sketches and elevation renderings that lead to digital & physical scale models and, finally, floor plans and a build-out.

**The fact is that space is internalized physically and emotionally.** As early as possible, find ways to experience the physicality and the emotional impact of the potential space. In the reality of project management and execution, this allows you to make decisions from experience. We've found experience to be a far more powerful compass than reason or conjecture.

**Prototyping is not a cheat, nor is it a work-around for those who lack vision.**
Even the best architects—those whose profession depends on the ability to intuit three dimensions from two-dimensional drawings—are surprised at how a building feels when it is completed. That, coupled with the purely financial approach of minimizing risky expenditures with low-cost early testing, is as rational a reason as any in support of working big early.

## see also

### 53
Design Template_Attitudes: Prototype toward a Solution

### 108
Tools_Full-Scale Space Prototyping Toolkit

Foam Cubes, Z-Racks, and tape lines arranged to test variations in room size for future faculty offices & student gathering spaces.

# Use Space to Level Status.

**Used thoughtfully, space can equalize status relationships and lay the groundwork for good ideas to emerge from surprising places.**

**Traditionally, space signals status.**
Imagine the pope in the ornate pulpit at St Peter's Basilica or a CEO's well-appointed corner office with a view overlooking Central Park in Manhattan.

**Leveling the status of individuals creates fertile ground for ideas to emerge from within a group.**
There may be plenty of good reasons to preserve a status hierarchy, but innovation requires the best ideas to carry the day—and these ideas can and should come from anywhere or anyone.

Level status by addressing elevation and arrangements:

**Literally put everyone on the same level.**
In teaching scenarios, platforms create a threshold that is hard to cross: teachers remain teachers, students remain students. Go even further and provide tall stools for students so they sit at eye-level with teachers standing amidst the crowd.

**Avoid arrangements that include "places of honor."**
Sit in circles and gather around square tables. The symmetry implies that all positions are equal. If a room naturally has a "place of honor" (such as the head of a table), let a lower-status individual sit there.

**Mix things up.**
Have students sit next to teachers, and put executives next to floor workers.

Distribute resources to teams or groups rather than to individuals.

## see also

22
Insights_Context Is Content

90
Insights_Special Touches Create a Sense of Belonging

Remains of
the Berlin Wall
in 2007.

# Space Is Not Always the Solution.

Space can be a pretty blunt instrument when it comes to addressing more nuanced subtleties in an organization. Because it is so blunt, it can lead to a bunch of unintended side effects.

**Existentialist philosopher Jean-Paul Sartre famously wrote, "Hell is other people."***
Maybe Jean-Paul was being a tad dramatic, but let's be honest: a lot of interpersonal conflict stirs up when you place people together, particularly under the stresses of a creative environment, where egos are repeatedly laid bare.

**Using space as a solution to nuanced social needs can damage culture.**
Example: The Corner Office. Individual offices have long been a method for communicating status and reward. In a highly collaborative organization, however, these offices often sit idle as their occupants spend time working with others on- or offsite. The walls then become a stale monument to what were perhaps valid desires to commemorate contribution and illuminate status, signaling to others that such space is more valuable in stillness than actively incorporated elsewhere.

**Use nonspace solutions when needed.**
Example: Celebrating the Host. Another subtlety that gives individuals a strong sense of ownership in the community is the ability to act as a host—when guests feel inspired, the host feels pride. Hosting status should be integrated into space design, through display of the host's work and access to amenities like kitchens and lounges, but often simply congratulating the host in front of his or her guests is the most effective way to honor the host's position in the community.

**Collaboration is hard. You need help.**
Dr. Julian Gorodsky, the "d.shrink," is a full-time psychologist who has worked with staff and students since the founding of the d.school. His work has validated the importance of directly addressing the realities of collaboration beyond buzzwords and trends. Embracing this approach has saved us the mental and monetary expense of constructing many walls.

*Jean-Paul Sartre, "No Exit" (1944).

see also

51
Design Template_Attitudes:
Collaborate across Boundaries

90
Insights_Special Touches Create a Sense of Belonging

# Build Empathy by Exploring All Angles.

**When redesigning a space, take the time to investigate different paths for different angles of view.**
How would you navigate the space if you were entering it for the first time to deliver a package? As an investor arriving for a meeting, how welcome would you feel? As you assume different roles, make sure to enter and exit the space at different locations. How would you redesign the different routes in response to these roles?

**The physical experience of "walking the lot" is critical in identifying the details that will make a difference.**
Architects often spend a great deal of time understanding how a building should sit on a lot to capitalize on the view or the light at different times of day. This process is no different for designers of space. Physically exploring the paths, sight lines, and obstacles by stepping through the space with an intent in mind—finding a bathroom, giving a tour, heading to the kitchen, shaking off your umbrella, or parking your bike—is a nonobvious, but fruitful, approach in designing the stories for your space.

see also

108
Tools_Full-Scale Space Prototyping Toolkit

114
Insights_Work Big Early

The Scoop Stool
is a multipurpose tool
for defining
collaboration spaces.

scoop
stool

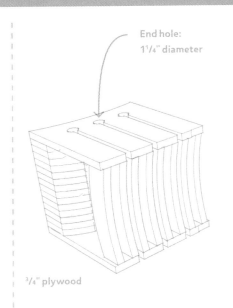

End hole:
1¼" diameter

"Scoop"
depth:
1½"

Short-term seating:
25- to 35-minute
duration

18"

18"

18"

¾" plywood

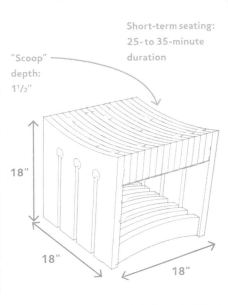

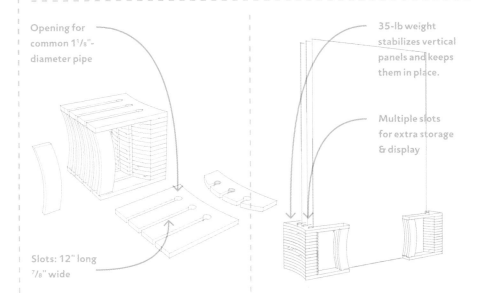

Opening for
common 1⅛"-
diameter pipe

Slots: 12" long
⅞" wide

35-lb weight
stabilizes vertical
panels and keeps
them in place.

Multiple slots
for extra storage
& display

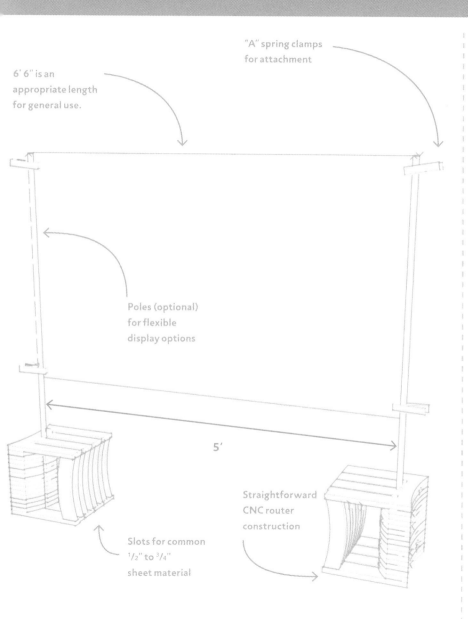

6' 6" is an appropriate length for general use.

"A" spring clamps for attachment

Poles (optional) for flexible display options

5'

Slots for common ¹/₂" to ³/₄" sheet material

Straightforward CNC router construction

The Scoop Stool supports a "pop-up" team space built around a single type of furniture. Its surfaces can be used for seating or minimal horizontal work, and the slots can hold panels (foamboard, polycarbonate, cardboard, etc.) for vertical work & display.

The Scoop Stool works as either an individual stool or, when grouped, as a bench. Use two stools to cradle the edges of work panels to store and display multiple sheets—you have a file organizer for team-scale work. The slot openings can accommodate pipes or poles to create additional infrastructure for a team space.

## sourcing

Rob Bell at Zomadic, LLC (San Francisco, CA; www.zomadic.com) constructed the Scoop Stools.

## see also

### 20
Situations_Instant /Shared Studio

### 150
Tools_Bulk Sheet Materials

### 162
Insights_Use Seats to Set a Time Limit

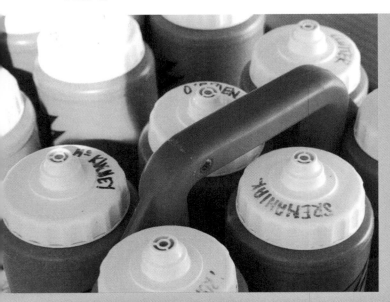

# Small Changes Can Have a Profound Impact.

**Example: water bottles**

The U.S. National Soccer Team came to Stanford to prepare for the 2010 Olympics in Beijing. The Stanford women's assistant soccer coach, Jay Cooney, spent some time with the U.S. coaching staff at practice.

One small thing Coach Cooney noticed was that the U.S. team uses a cart of water bottles instead of a communal watercooler to rehydrate the players during breaks. He saw the impact this had on the players and immediately switched from using a cooler with cups to a cart with prefilled water bottles.

What he saw was this: the bottle cart was simultaneously accessible to all players. A cooler with cups allows only one or two players at a time to use it, while the rest split off, diffusing team camaraderie. Accessible from all angles, the bottle cart afforded the players an opportunity to hang out and chat. Jay seized even this subtle opportunity to enhance team cohesion and communication.

**Example: making or breaking start-ups**

At 500 Startups, an early-stage venture capital fund and accelerator in the heart of Silicon Valley, 20 new start-up teams work intensely side by side. Teams face either outside through windows or inward toward work spaces and walkways. Seating orientation relative to visitors can be high stakes, as potential investors often hang out in the space.

A remark from one of the start-up's CEOs to Enrique Allen, the founding designer at 500 Startups, initiated a change in the space: "I love meeting great people serendipitously—that's one of the big benefits of being here. But when someone comes by our desks, even for a few minutes, they distract our whole team."

To solve this conundrum, the CEO simply rearranged the orientation of desks in a "U" shape, putting teammates who did the most coding (and thus required sustained focus) next to windows, and putting himself in front of the major walkway to greet important visitors. These minor adjustments in orientation allowed the team to protect precious development time and take advantage of opportunistic encounters with potential investors.

see also

44
Design Template_Properties: Orientation

# Use Soft Boundaries to Partition Open Spaces.

**Eliminating walls and opaque partitioning is one of the first significant steps in creating "flexible" collaborative spaces.**
When walls are gone, boundaries become even more important; the need for transition space like hallways does not vanish in the absence of the walls that shaped it.

**Ignoring the intent & effect of partitions can be one of the great downfalls of an "open" space.**
People seek boundaries and edges indoors and out. Couple this tendency with cued boundaries such as floor striping, contrasting-color floors, different flooring materials, and low partitions to create highly effective pseudo-walls that function almost like actual walls.

Proof of the power of soft boundaries can be found on any street or sports court you see. Check out the relationship between a bicyclist and a motorist on opposite sides of a painted stripe: life literally depends on the agreement that a single painted line will not be violated.

see also

217
Insights_Use Limits to Inspire Creativity

245
Insights_Flooring Shapes Creative Activities

# project
# rooms

start

Low budget: Commandeer a small, unused office or conference room: (100–200 sq ft). Assign it to a team for a project. Encourage team members to plaster the walls with their work. See what happens.

Big budget: Same as above—plus strategically replace one opaque wall with a transparent surface (glass, acrylic, polycarbonate) for maximum visibility into the space.

**A Project Room is a space for a small team to meet in and saturate with project stuff—inspiration, illustrations, and work in progress.**
A project room works like an apartment rental: it's inhabited by a team during a project. When the project is completed, the room is passed along to the next team.

**Important features:**

**Lots of usable wall space.**
Creative teams thrive when surrounded by stuff related to the project. Any and all available wall space should be filled with inspirational photos, empathetic quotes gathered in the field, data, sketches, maps, and whatever inspirational artifacts keep team members focused on the challenge. Writable (e.g., dry-erase whiteboard) and mountable (e.g., magnetic boards) surfaces are key.

**Maximum visibility with minimum interruption.**
We love to see people at work—it lets you know who's around and contributes an energetic feel to the space. On the flip side, when jamming on a project, we don't like being distracted. Use glass walls that are frosted at eye level. A cheaper and equally pleasing option is to use clear, ribbed polycarbonate sheets to skin a wall (one popular architectural product goes by the name Polygal). The ribs reveal color, light, and motion without detail or eye contact.

**A little acoustic privacy.**
Acoustic privacy is good for obvious reasons: noise is distracting, and sometimes we want to say something to just one person and nobody else. However, letting go of just a little of that privacy comes with collateral benefits. "Just enough" acoustic dampening renders conversations largely unintelligible but lets some sound through to add to the ambient energy of the space. Also, wall construction & HVAC systems can be installed with less expensive "broad strokes," versus more costly fine tuning.

see also

26
Tools_HACK: Showerboard Dry-Erase Surface

150
Tools_Bulk Sheet Materials

204
Situations_Meeting Place

# Palomar5: Exploring the Space between Work and Life

## by Maryanna Rogers

**Complete freedom within sharp confines**

I am a designer, researcher, and artist. So, naturally, the opportunity to become a resident at the Palomar5 (P5) innovation camp enticed me. While there, I would join "29 youngsters"— international entrepreneurs, scientists, hackers, artists—to generate and share ideas about the future of work. Noticeably absent from this call were details about what it would actually be like during our seven-week "exploration of creative space." For instance, I didn't realize the term "sleeping box" meant I would be spending each night in the same subdivided room as thirty-five strangers. Needless to say, we became close very quickly.

Just after we arrived from our fourteen different home countries, the P5 team took a hands-off approach and declared that we residents would collectively make decisions about how we would create collaborative projects on the topic of "the future of work." Other details, however, were thoroughly designed, right down to our bright blue P5 jumpsuits.

## "On" and "Off"

At the end of week one, project teams began to coalesce. One team chose to explore designing work spaces to accommodate different mindsets—when we are "On" and when we are "Off." According to the team's stance, there should be distinct spaces of active work and moments of rest. This particular project was abandoned after a couple of weeks, but a look at the campers themselves is insightful: did residents need discrete spaces for being "On" and "Off" in a radical live-work environment?

## Live-work, work-live spaces

The P5 live-work experience was housed in an artfully renovated 2,000-square-meter malt factory on the southern edge of Berlin. The main co-working room was sliced up by an architectural structure ("The White Cube"), which divided the expansive space into smaller quarters that flowed into and out of each other. The sleeping boxes, that were just large enough for

a built-in cot and tiny closet, were well designed, featuring a door and a small porch with a roll-down translucent screen for privacy. Other common areas included a dining room, a kitchen, a prototyping and presentation room ("p-room"), and an entertainment room. All of these rooms became spaces for formal team meetings and sessions alongside dance breaks, Guitar Hero, napping, cuddling, and hanging out.

left: "The White Cube"

right: Exterior of the malt factory

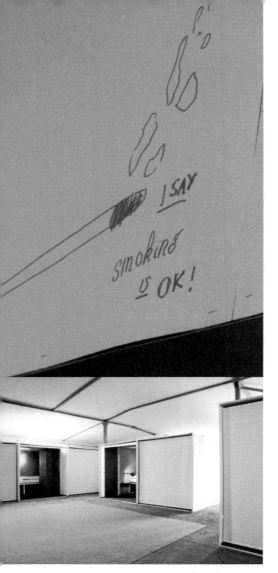

# Space Studies_Exploring the Space between Work and Life

top: Drawing
on the wall of the
smoking room

bottom: The
sleeping boxes

### Defining an "off" space

While most rooms at the camp were used for both work and play, one in particular, the smoking room, was decidedly an "off" space—a safe zone. Residents gathered here in clouds of smoke to have open-ended conversations related to both projects and personal matters. One resident who had doubts about her creative abilities finally found the courage and comfort necessary to try building something for the first time here. Fittingly, it was an ashtray—with wheels.

The outdoor smoking area also served a special function. One resident, after deciding to abandon her project idea, joined a friend for a cigarette. Her smoking buddy confided that he really liked the project and thought it would be a shame if she dropped it. "Without me saying anything he just told me that he thinks it's really sad that we killed that project. He thinks we should bring it back to life." His words made an impression on her; she resumed the project. Although it seemed superficial, the discussion triggered a pivotal shift—restarting a stalled project. The context of this conversation was critical—the informality of the smoke break created permission for free discussion.

### The relevance of the P5 experience to real-world design teams

Designers often investigate "extreme cases" to uncover needs that apply across different populations but are more difficult to identify in less extreme contexts. The behaviors that emerged at the camp, in a context of "extreme collaboration"* and "radical co-location"† not unlike the atmospheres of many start-ups, illuminate widely relevant design opportunities.

Although they were clearly "off" spaces, the smoking areas at the camp seemed to fulfill a special role in the creative process—they were safe spaces that gave residents courage to try something new and permission to voice personal opinions about work. In doing so, they often dramatically altered and accelerated the course of our work.

Though somewhat unorthodox in setting, the work and play practices at the camp suggest that the "On/Off" team may have been onto something: in intensely collaborative work environments that require long days (and nights) of work, spaces designed not to support do work serve functional purpose.

Palomar5 residents
discussing
project work.

* Shaw, B. G. (2007). More than the Sum of the Parts: Shared Representations in Collaborative Design Interaction (Doctoral dissertation). Royal College of Art, London, UK.
† Teasley, S.D., Covi, L., Krishnan, M.S., & Olson, J.S. (2000). How does radical collocation help a team succeed? Proceedings of CSCW 2000. New York: ACM Press. 339–346.

Maryanna Rogers is a designer, artist, and researcher. Her art work focuses on interactions among data and electronic media. Her research focuses on the intersection of design and education.

hack

see-through
walls

# Both visual transparency & acoustic privacy are important in collaborative spaces.

Visual overlap elevates the energy of being able to see others, while acoustic separation eliminates the distraction of overlapping conversations. Glass is an ideal medium for both situations, but glass walls can get expensive.

Here are two cheaper alternatives. Neither of these alternatives offers perfect acoustic separation for private conversation, but both work to dampen distraction. Some people prefer partial acoustic separation: the ability to hear some ambient sound is a reminder of nearby activities. Those who have something to hide tend to get a little concerned.

## build instructions

**Option 1:**

1. Clear walls on the cheap: drywall with see-through skins.

2. Before beginning, take appropriate precautions.*

3. Remove the drywall on both sides of the wall.

4. Purchase 4' x 8' sheets of $1/16$"-thick polycarbonate to replace the drywall

5. Cut the polycarbonate sheets to size so the seams are aligned on the now-exposed wall studs.

**Option 2:**

1. Poke some holes in it.
This can be fun, but be careful.*

2. Knock holes out between the studs on the wall.

3. Finish out the insides of the holes with drywall or make them into "aquariums," using polycarbonate. Size & shape are up to you. Consider sight lines and height.

4. Finish the edges with spackle.

5. Prime & repaint.

## tips

**Option 1:**

· Have the polycarbonate cut by the vendor or use a jigsaw with a fine-tooth blade and a guide.
· Use self-drilling screws with wide heads; run them along the joints of abutted sheets.

**Option 2:**

· Find wall studs with a stud finder (accurate) or by tapping on the wall to listen for dead spots (not so accurate). The dead spots indicate where the studs are located.

*Important! When removing drywall, poking holes in walls, and tweaking any infrastructure, be careful! Modifying load-bearing walls can be trouble. Walls hide electrical conduit containing the wiring that powers everything around you. Don't do anything to any walls before you know their structural function in the building around you. Also, consult the relevant building codes: the use of polycarbonate, for example, might not fit the fire code for your area. Before you start the work, always take the extra safety precaution of turning off the electricity to the area in which you are working at the circuit breaker.

## sourcing

**polycarbonate/acrylic**
Port Plastics (550 East Trimble Road, San Jose, CA 95131; 408 571-2231; www.portplastics.com) ships regionally.
TAP Plastics (154 South Van Ness, San Francisco, CA 94103; 800 246-5055; www.tapplastics.com)

**Instant infrastructure for creating team spaces and writing surfaces.**

The T-Walls (so called because of their shape on a floor plan) allow for the creation of rapid configurations of intimate or open spaces in any context. They are one of the most time-tested elements at the d.school. An early need to be able to quickly adapt spaces for multiple-use cases had us literally mounting entire walls on casters to move them about the space.

Each T-Wall unit consists of two nearly identical "walls." These walls are wood frames "skinned" with thinner laminate materials such as acrylic, polycarbonate, Masonite, and showerboard. The nonporous surfaces of showerboard and acrylic, for example, create easily replaceable, dry-erase writable surfaces—less expensive than commercially available products of similar scale.

The framing construction can be basic, using standard 2x4 lumber, or more elaborate, using thick (1") multi-ply plywood or finer hardwood lumber.

# t-walls

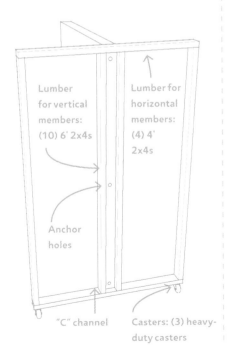

Lumber for vertical members: (10) 6' 2x4s

Lumber for horizontal members: (4) 4' 2x4s

Anchor holes

"C" channel

Casters: (3) heavy-duty casters

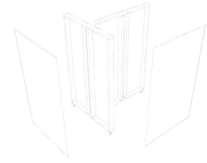

Overall height: 6' 6"
Showerboard surfacing specs: (4) sheets @ 4' x 6' 3".

Hardware:
Self-tapping lath screws for showerboard attachment at 8" spacings.

Carriage bolts (with nuts & washers) or lag screws for connecting wall components

## build instructions

**build sequence:**

1. Build the frames.

2. Skin one side of each as illustrated.

3. Connect the walls.

4. Attach remaining skins.

5. Install casters anytime after Step 1.

**the guts**
Both wall components are identical, with a consistent C-shaped vertical center assembly, allowing either wall to function as connector for the pair, using bolts or lag screws. Holes for these bolts or screws should be predrilled in the center channel before installing the laminate surface; holes should be located at top, mid, and bottom heights.

**how tall?**
We have found 6' 6" to be a good height for usability without intimidation. Taller surfaces can wreck team dynamics and create unreachable areas.

## sourcing

**showerboard/lumber**
Lumber & showerboard are available from local lumber suppliers as well as home centers. The d.school has had excellent results with the product available from
Pine Cone Lumber (895 East Evelyn Avenue, Sunnyvale, CA 94086; 408 736-5491; www.pineconelumber.com).

**casters**
Industrial Caster & Wheel Co. (2200 Carden Street, San Leandro, CA 94577; 510 569-8303; www.icwco.com). Reference Stanford d.school red caster in 3" or 5".
California Caster and Hand Truck Company (1400 17th Street, San Francisco, CA 94107; 800 950-8750; www.californiacaster.com)

**polycarbonate/acrylic**
Port Plastics (550 East Trimble Road, San Jose, CA 95131; 408 571-2231; www.portplastics.com) ships regionally.
TAP Plastics (154 South Van Ness, San Francisco, CA 94103; 800 246-5055; www.tapplastics .com) has many western U.S. locations.

## start

Because it is a tall, rolling structure, the T-Wall needs to be built sturdily. Start with a quantity of one or two (a pair is nice) and use the cheap option: standard 2x4s.

## see also

**16**
Tools_Z-Rack

**58**
Tools_Whiteboard Sliders

Common configurations for using T-Walls with teams.

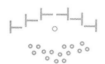

"Lecture"

"In the Round"

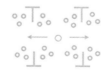

"Expo"

"On Stage"

# hiding place

**Hiding places offer a crucial respite from an open, collaborative environment.**
The more extroverted the work space, the more you need these spots of passive, dark yin amid the swaths of hyperactive, brightly lit yang. Few offices have legitimate hiding places; if your space lacks one, people will go elsewhere to find it.

**What makes a good hiding place?**
At the d.school, we created a space we call "Booth Noir" as a response to the need for a place to get away. Deconstructing Booth Noir reveals critical characteristics of any good hiding place:

**It's different.**
It stands in stark contrast to the rest of the space and offers a needed break.

**It's immovable.**
The furniture in the room is fixed to the floor and walls. There are no decisions to be made, nothing to arrange but your own posture.

**It's beyond low-tech—it's no tech.**
Outlets, switches, and data jacks are hidden from view.

**It's tiny: 8' x 8'.**
Small scale encourages feelings of coziness & security.

**It's dark, yet warm.**
It's devoid of the bright colors that streak walls in other spaces. Current codes often require high-efficiency lighting fixtures (generally fluorescents). Rebel by installing an incandescent floor lamp. This helps—a lot!

**It's laid back.**
A large bench inside encourages—even requires—reclining and relaxing

**It's hidden.**
It's tucked away in a corner on the ground floor. The only reason to go there is to go there; it's not on the way to anywhere else.

**It smells good—or, at least, different.**
The furniture is made from fragrant cedar. The distinctive aroma heightens the other senses.

**It requires a ritual to enter.**
A sign on the door handle asks visitors to remove their shoes. The simple gesture of taking off your shoes breaks your routine—and the cedar fragrance does a good job of masking foot odor.

## start

Choose a metaphor for your relaxation space: spa, yoga studio, bedroom, Zen garden, etc. Identify some of the properties that make this metaphorical space relaxing—a place to lie down, soft music, natural light—and use them as inspirations in implementing your own hiding place with available resources or some inexpensive purchases (e.g., throw rugs, incandescent lamps). Avoid items that don't wear well like dainty pillows or superplush fabrics. If the space is enjoyed often, spend a little more money to make it sing.

## see also

**45**
Design Template_Properties: Ambience

**89**
Insights_Build in Little Rituals

**Booth Noir:**
a hiding place
at the d.school.

make space

Dreamhost office, Brea, CA. Designed by Studio O+A. Design Team: Primo Orpilla, Verda Alexander, Denise Cherry, Kroeun Dav, Alfred Socias, Alexander Ng.

# Design Strong Points & Counterpoints.

Great spaces are often great because they amplify a particular character, but such specialized spaces aren't able to service every need.

In an open and highly collaborative environment, extroversion and activity are encouraged. The counterpoints are introversion, reflection, and introspection. Large, open space should always have smaller, closable spaces available nearby to provide privacy and escape.
Identifying the point and

counterpoint relationships in both spaces provides exciting opportunities to amplify the details that scream one thing or another: make your open spaces expansive like a sports arena and confine your closed spaces like a London phone booth.

**Consistency of intent creates coherency, while variation in execution creates delight.** It is important to provide a sense of place and to create a holistically supportive environment, but include variations on the theme. These variations can be as simple as different flooring from room to room or full-scale thematic variation among multiple rooms of the same type—if you have two conference rooms, create

one called the "conference room" and one called the "anti–conference room." Contrasting or varied choices can help activity leaders design a unique experience with minimal effort. The tone for a gathering can then be set by a simple choice of venue.

## see also

# Leave a Room Clean or Messy?

**A fresh & clean space lies ready and waiting for a team and its work, but a space scattered with lingering ideas and artifacts hints at potential.** Stanford Archaeology Professor Michael Shanks calls the latter "[part of] a visual history of the room."

There is a tricky balance between stimulating creation and squelching new work with old clutter. Like Goldilocks looking for the just-right porridge, teams seem to instinctively find resonance in a room that is "just clean enough." More than a just few minutes spent straightening up a room are too many, but walking into a stark white room lined with whiteboards that show no trace of writing can feel bleak and daunting. A few ghostly remnants of erased writing can jump-start the next engagement by signaling behavior.

To some people, a little mess is permission for more, while others find the slightest mess to be as distracting and unprofessional as walking into a meeting with your pants down. Trying out a few "rules for behavior" and actively monitoring the results is a good way to zero in on a happy medium.

## see also

102
Insights_Enter on Action

197
Insights_The Responsibility-Adjustability Slide Rule

203
Insights_Patina Gives Permission

**Printmaking studio at Crown Point Press, San Francisco, CA.**

# Help People Cope with Change.

**As you design spaces for and within an existing community, you'll also have to take on the burden of easing change.**

**Design is more than an agent of change, it is change.**
Space designers change everything that a person experiences—in three dimensions, no less. While change is exciting for some, it is positively terrifying for others. As shiny and hopeful as it is, a new space also threatens status and arouses nostalgia for the way things were.

The d.school's repeated moves reveal a pretty predictable cycle: in the first couple of months following a move there is palpable excitement for the new, followed three months later by an equally intense nostalgia for the old. People then rebel a bit, making their own marks on the new space, and eventually they begin to emotionally invest in the new building. Another nine months later, we move again and the cycle repeats.

We don't claim to have a formula to assuage anxiety around change, but we have identified some techniques that help:

**Start small.** Change is difficult when it's perceived as permanent. Try things out at a small scale before implementing at a large scale (e.g., experiment with a corner before rearranging a classroom).

**Give the community a chance to experience the change.** This is key. Prototype at full scale—mock up the space. People build apprehensions when they compare a known with an unknown. Calm their nerves with opportunities to get to know the future through prototypes.

**Get others involved.** Create opportunities for people to physically build and contribute concepts. When people participate in the process, they begin forging an emotional bond with the space.

**Incorporate rites of passage.** We've christened new buildings by smashing champagne bottles, sacrificed prototypes from the cliffs of loading docks, and bestowed ceremonial keys upon our community. As silly as they might seem, rituals work.

**Be authentic.** Tell people what's happening, not what you think they want to hear. If things are behind schedule, let them know.

**Communicate what's needed, at the right time.** Maintain a bias toward openness, but design is a tumultuous process and there is no need to share every detail at every moment. A good rule of thumb is to share information when you find yourself speculating about input or opinions from others.

**Absorb feedback.** Taking in and responding to feedback are crucial activities in an iterative process: they help you make the right change. Listen to everything with both an open mind and a critical ear. There are often hidden messages behind every suggestion: it is up to you to decide which should inform your trajectory.

## see also

Recreation of World War II era poster designed to be deployed in anticipation of a large-scale attack on British soil. It was never distributed, but has found new meaning in reprints.

Immediately accessible
portable projection
and sound.

# lanterns

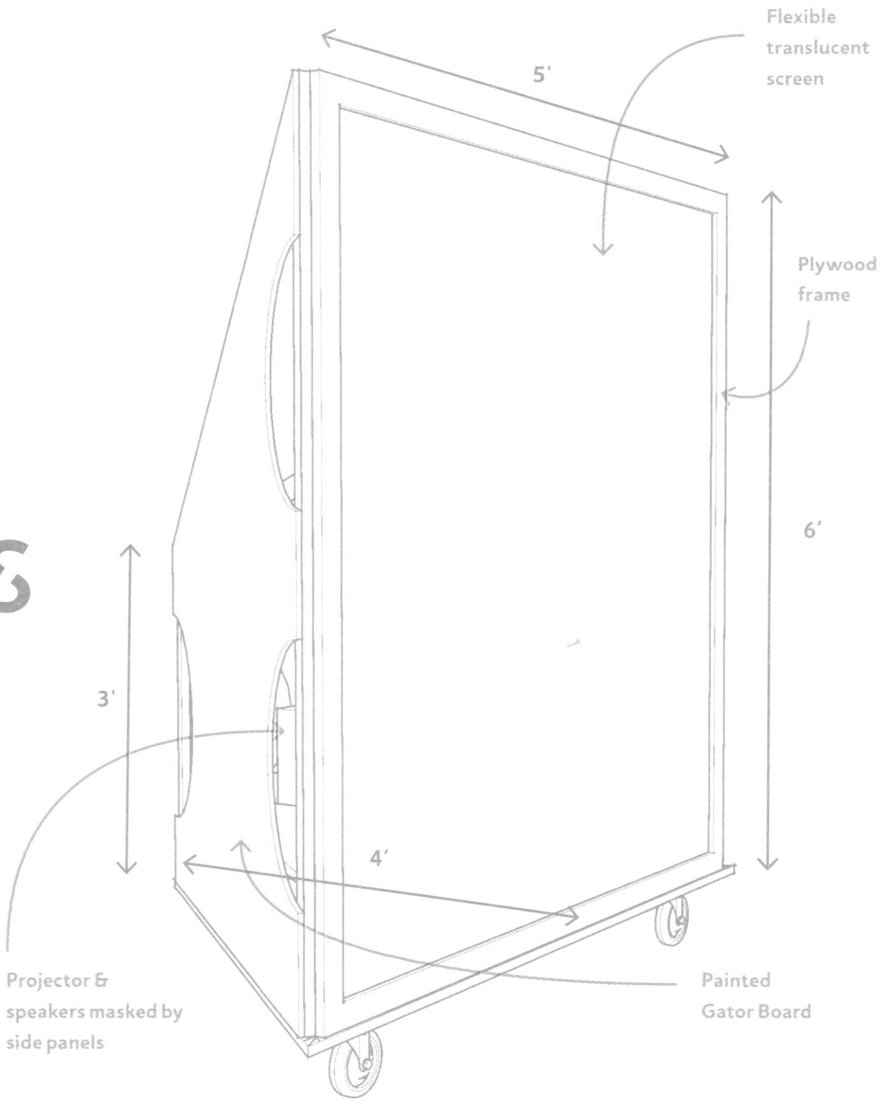

Flexible
translucent
screen

Plywood
frame

5'

6'

3'

4'

Projector &
speakers masked by
side panels

Painted
Gator Board

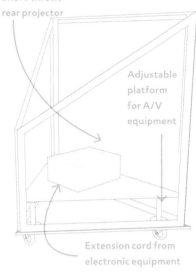

Short-throw, rear projector

Adjustable platform for A/V equipment

Extension cord from electronic equipment

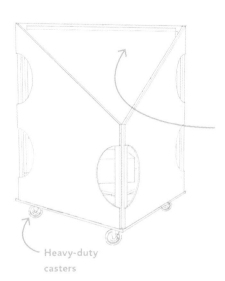

Acrylic back panel creates a "glow"

Heavy-duty casters

Lanterns are self-contained carts that house a short-throw rear-projector and a speaker system. Starting a presentation requires essentially no setup: plug a Lantern into an electrical outlet, plug a source (e.g., laptop computer) into the Lantern projector, and begin.

Lanterns are ideal for activity-based experiences in which temporary projection might be helpful: in a hallway, in an open space away from walls, or in a kitchen.

Unlike large, heavy monitors built into dark metal and plastic housings, Lanterns are lightweight carts built of simple materials: plywood, vinyl, foamboard. They can be used in any location and, unlike large monitors, they maneuver easily, thus constituting a less dominating presence when not in use.

Simple connections and minimal materials make Lanterns easy to disassemble. You can easily reconfigure them with new & updated equipment as specific technologies advance.

## start

The spirit of the Lanterns can be achieved by having portable projectors readily available. Couple a portable sound system with a projector mounted on a furniture dolly as a practical first step.

## sourcing

**manufacturing**
Lanterns were designed at the d.school and constructed by Because We Can (2500 Kirkham Street, Oakland, CA 94607; 510 922-8846; www.becausewecan.org).

## see also

### 96
Insights_Make Technology Radically Accessible, But Don't Use It Often

# frosted polyester film mini-screens

## Hang this durable material and project an image onto it that virtually floats in midair.

The frosted polyester film mini-screen is a quick & inexpensive alternative to commercial screens or a custom screen. Don't worry about the word polyester: no wide-collar disco shirts here. Just a durable material that isn't easily destroyed.

The polyester material in question is really boPET—biaxially oriented polyethylene terephthalate. Whew! There are many trade names for this product, including Mylar. Many different types of material will work for this application: try any semitranslucent material, frosted acrylic, or even thin, white bedsheets.

## build instructions

Find plastic or polyester material that won't rip or stain easily.

Go as big as possible. Make sure the dimensions are in a 4:3 or 16:9 ratio to match the projection. Some sheets are available in 40" x 30" size: this is perfect.

Hang with fishing line and transparent tape to enhance the floating effect.

Weigh down the bottom by attaching weights or a metal dowel.

## tip

· If you use bedsheets, iron them, unless wrinkles are part of your intended effect.

## sourcing

You can find many sources for plastic and polyester sheets online.

Grafix Plastics is one reliable supplier. Grafix Plastics (5800 Pennsylvania Ave., Cleveland, OH 44317; www.grafixplastics.com)

## see also

84
Tools_Hanging Screen

# Corners Provide a Sense of Place.

**The slightest hint of a corner has a profound effect on the sense of ownership in an open space.**
Two perpendicular walls provide a suggestion of an edge that outlines a space. These perceived boundaries are easy to absorb, navigate, populate, and protect.

It doesn't take much. In one of the early d.school space prototypes, student teams with access to corner spots spent far more time in the space working on their projects than teams whose spaces were on an open wall. In a second prototype space, featuring side-by-side team spaces with partial corners, we interviewed students and found that a corner with a side wall projecting as little as 1' sufficed to provide a feeling of comfort in the space.*

\* Research conducted by Adam Royalty, Lead Research Investigator at the Stanford d.school.

## see also

**121**
Insights_Use Soft Boundaries to Partition Open Spaces

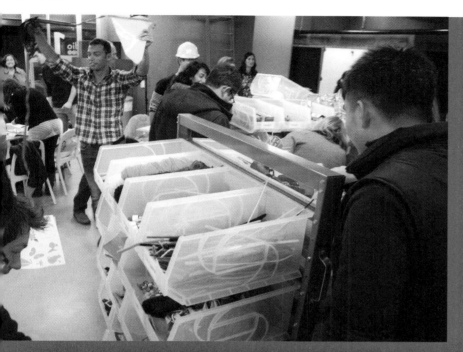

**Ample work space and radically accessible tools.**
Providing space to use tools and materials is as important as those objects themselves. Ample work surfaces and opportunities to make and display physical embodiments—whether robots, paper prototypes, or digital experiences—encourage people to create. Tools do, too: keep hand tools, soldering stuff, and electronics equipment around in equal measure with fasteners and fixtures such as clamps and vises, so that people actually can build rather than just thinking about what they wish they had.

*Björn Hartmann, Scott Doorley, Scott Klemmer, "Hacking, Mashing, Gluing: Understanding Opportunistic Design," Pervasive Computing, July–September 2008.

# Keep Supplies & Tools Visible for Inspiration & Instruction.

**People get inspired by what's around them. Surround them with inspiration.**
Take cues from toy designers: they engulf themselves with piles of inspirational junk, from simple balls to programmable microcontrollers.* These bits and pieces pilfered from the guts of other toys are ready to be crammed into new configurations.

**"Out of sight, out of mind."**
There is truth to the old cliché. Enhancing access to supplies & tools is absolutely crucial, as people tend to engage with only those items that are near at hand. Showcasing materials and supplies accelerates the potential for those magical moments of creative inspiration.

## see also

# adjustable flare/focus spaces

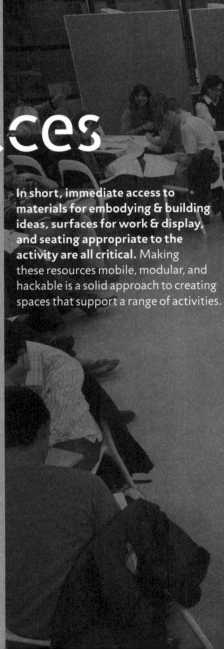

**Collaboration can shift
from a hush to a scream
in a moment.**
When teams are flaring, or generating
ideas they might be physically standing,
moving around, and building things.
When teams are focusing they will
often be gathered tightly in a group or
circled around displays of artifacts and
information. Charting the changes in
behavior is an excellent approach to
tailoring resources: each action offers
a clue. Shifting from flaring to focusing
can take place instantaneously, yet they
are very different activities that require
very different support.

**Keep flaring supplies
and surfaces at hand.**
An idea pops up and someone wants to
draw it. Always have writing materials
within reach—dry-erase boards, pens,
paper, Post-its . . . something. A team
needs to storyboard a presentation.
Vertical surfaces should be ready to
receive the attention. It should be convenient to move chairs out of the way.

**Use adjustable walls
or flexible seating alternatives
to enable a shift into focus.**
Key to creating the intimacy required
for focusing activities are the ability to
limit distraction and to calmly connect
with others. A team needs to pause and
reflect. Seats to support the reflective
mode should be available nearby—a
move from standing to sitting often
signals a shift from flaring to focusing.
Partitions (such as the Z-Rack) that
can be adjusted to block sight lines and
shrink the space provide barriers to
distraction and make perceived space
seem more intimate.

**In short, immediate access to
materials for embodying & building
ideas, surfaces for work & display,
and seating appropriate to the
activity are all critical.** Making
these resources mobile, modular, and
hackable is a solid approach to creating
spaces that support a range of activities.

## start

Rather than trying to support every possible shift in activity, focus first on high-contrast shifts—transitioning from seated & talking to standing & building, for example. Try setting up adjacent accommodations for both activities (e.g., low seats and footrests next to worktables without seats). Get comfortable with the major shifts and then spend more time & attention on additional options.

## see also

# Cutting into Corporate Culture

## by Tom Maiorana

Space Studies_Cutting into Corporate Culture

I am not a space designer, but as a designer and consultant I have seen the impact that space can have on creativity. I work in a large company that values and supports innovation but has very few spaces that foster creativity. With that in mind, I thought it would be fun to see if I could do something to make our typical corporate setting a bit more interesting.

I should mention that I'm impatient, scattered, and not all that politically savvy. Knowing this, I felt my best shot at getting anything done without getting fired was to go outside the sanctioned channels and start small. I made sixteen-inch cubes to be used for seats, tables, or props in skits and experience prototypes. It seemed the simplest way to change a space.

My plan was to use these for our internal design thinking workshops. Given that context, I set a few constraints for the cubes—they had to be nonpermanent, assemble in less than ten minutes, and cost less than $50 for a set of five. At first these rules felt arbitrary— something to do to make the project successful, but they quickly became something more. The constraints kept me on task and helped me focus on a simple, concrete goal. Without them, I'd surely have a pile of sketches but none of the real feedback or learning that comes with bringing something—even something very simple—to completion.

Shifting from digital to physical output was the first hurdle. With

interaction design, nearly all of my work is "clean." Software doesn't damage my clothing. It won't cut me. Regardless of how badly I screw up, I'm never more than a few keystrokes from undoing my mistakes. So even the slight shift to cutting cardstock with a utility knife changes all that.

I'm no stranger to making physical objects, so I recognize that it necessitates a different mindset and requires real time and effort. In many ways it's akin to what Paul Graham, co-founder of the venture capital firm

above: Interior support structure for cardboard cube seat prototype.

Y Combinator, describes as a maker's schedule. Makers need blocks of time to get deep into a problem. This is true of developers and interaction designers, as well as makers of small cardboard cubes.

In corporate culture, PowerPoint decks are the norm, and most of them are visual train wrecks. Despite that fact, they can feel more refined than a well-considered but roughly executed physical object (especially to colleagues who aren't used to seeing early-stage physical prototypes). When I first used the cubes in a workshop, I struggled with the fact that they appeared so shoddy compared to everything else in the polished corporate setting.

Rough does have its advantages, however. I got over my disappointment and brought the cubes in for a design thinking session with internal folks and our customers as well. We asked the participants to develop a prototype using any of the materials in the room. They paused, evaluating the Post-its, duct tape, and assorted materials. Then a woman picked up one of the cubes and asked, "Can I draw on this?" Of course! Roughness encouraged her to make the space her own, to ignore (or at least question) the rules, and to transform the "givens" into something entirely different. If our team can learn that it's okay to alter, break, hack, and tamper with our space, perhaps it'll further open up the way we think about our more traditional challenges. That's my hope anyway.

Corporations move slowly. Transforming your space probably isn't the most direct route to a raise. It's not the best way to get a promotion. But it is a great way to become a more fluid thinker, to get a visceral learning experience that you can apply to the rest of your job, and, if you're persistent, it might end up making a lasting impact on your organization.

Tom Maiorana is a product design strategist. He is a consultant to a variety of corporations, start-ups, and non-profits. His projects range from human factors understanding to product strategy and development.

right: Prepping the prototype in sequence.

Standard size for most materials is 4' x 8' from the manufacturer.

Stock the largest format your space can handle. Separate the stacks and keep the sheets neat.

# bulk sheet materials

¹/₄" foamboard is easy to cut—works great for building physical prototypes.

¹/₂" foamboard is stiff enough to use for presentation panels.

# Bulk sheet materials are great to have on hand for any stage of a design process.

These large-format surfaces can be used as components for building in all aspects, from on-the-fly team space infrastructure to raw materials for prototyping. Prop a panel against a wall and you have a principal work surface. Arrange several for a more saturated, immersive team space.

The following are some excellent lightweight & versatile materials:
· Foamboard as display & work surfaces for Post-its and printed photographs. In addition to its light weight, it is easy to cut and reusable.
· Rigid foamboard, called Gator Board, for very sturdy display and work surfaces. It's very strong, ensuring reusability.
· Corrugated polycarbonate works well as a reusable dry-erase writing surface & team space partition. It's sturdy, translucent, and unique.
· Butcher paper can be cut to any length for floor-to-ceiling or wall-to-wall work surfaces. It's plentiful and expendable.

## tips

· If you have the space, buy & store sheet materials at full size, usually 4' x 8', to preserve the maximum number of options for later use. Keep these fundamental tools on display and available for use.
· Keep A-shaped spring clamps & binder clips handy for mounting sheets to . . . anything.
· Order in bulk to save money.
· Make sure you have cutting tools handy (X-acto knives, saws, etc.).

## sourcing

**foamboard/cardboard**
Arch Supplies (99 Missouri, San Francisco, CA 94107; 415 433-2724; www.archsupplies.com)

**foamboard/gator board**
ULINE Shipping Supply Specialists (800 958-5463; www.uline.com)

**showerboard**
Showerboard is available at most home centers and local lumber suppliers.
Pine Cone Lumber (895 East Evelyn Avenue, Sunnyvale, CA 94086; 408 736-5491; www.pineconelumber.com)

**polycarbonate/acrylic**
Port Plastics (550 East Trimble Road, San Jose, CA 95131; 408 571-2231; www.portplastics.com) ships regionally.
TAP Plastics (154 South Van Ness, San Francisco, CA 94103; 800 246-5055; www.tapplastics .com) has many western U.S. locations.

## start

Order a back-stock of material. Keep it on display for use. Start with a stack leaning against an available wall. Next, try a rolling "lumber" cart. Then build a partitioned rack.

**paper**
Butcher paper, brown and white, in various dimensions:
Kelly Paper (1375 Howard Street, San Francisco, CA 94103; 415 522-0420; www.kellypaper .com) has many regional locations.

**plywood**
Local wood suppliers or home centers

## see also

Use lightweight panels as instant, permeable partitions.

# aesthetic panels

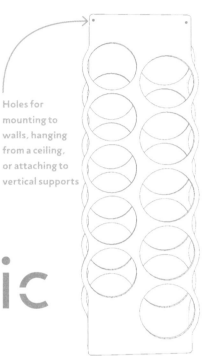

Holes for mounting to walls, hanging from a ceiling, or attaching to vertical supports

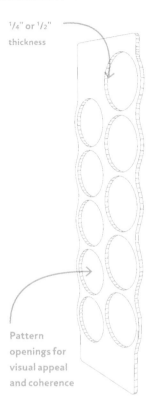

¹/₄" or ¹/₂" thickness

Pattern openings for visual appeal and coherence

Any regular pattern of holes works, but beware of busy-ness.

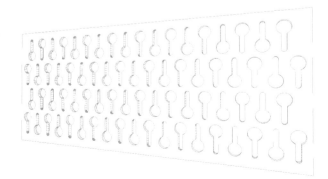

A simple plane of visual separation can be enough to allow a hallway to pass through a workspace without the burden of normal walls or cubicles.

Panels function like a porous picket fence: they draw intrigue by creating gaps through which neighbors can sneak a peek. That glimpse is often enough to communicate that someone is busy with work and shouldn't be disturbed. It also allows for an easy point of engagement: "Hey, that looks interesting! What are you doing?"

The panel pattern sets the aperture for access. Think of it this way: no panel equates to no separation. An opaque office is the equivalent of 100 percent separation. Patterned openings with large holes suggest separation but not privacy, while smaller or high & low openings discourage interruption.

Patterns on panels also transform the visual landscape within a space. Instead of functioning as partitions, align them along existing walls to influence the ambience of an environment.

Panel materials can be consistent or deliberately varied for additional effect. Use foamboard, Gator Board, plywood, or Masonite for easy-to-source and easy-to-modify sheet materials.

## build instructions

Make panels from almost any sheet material. Mount the panels to vertical supports; hang them from the ceiling; attach them to walls.

Gator Board and plywood can be mechanically cut using simple graphic files uploaded to cutting machinery (e.g., CNC router, waterjet cutter). This is a straightforward operation for local millworks.

Stickers and decals, either precut or designed in-house using a vinyl cutter, can be used to create excellent partitions when applied to transparent panels such as glass, acrylic, or polycarbonate.

Create a pattern graphic file (usually .dxf) to use as a "cut file" at a local CNC shop.

Opening dimensions vary with intent.
Large openings = public
Small openings = private

## start

Prototype Aesthetic Panel quantities & locations using large sheets of butcher paper. Cut patterns with an X-Acto knife to give you an idea of the impact created by patterned openings. These steps will save time & money prior to making more elaborate panels.

## sourcing

**foamboard/cardboard**
Arch Supplies (99 Missouri St., San Francisco, CA 94107; 415 433-2724; www.archsupplies.com

**foamboard/gator board**
ULINE Shipping Supply Specialists; 800 958-5463; www.uline.com

**plywood**
Plywood is perhaps the most durable material for easily constructed panels, but it is heavier than foamboard and Gator Board. Multi-ply plywood is readily available at home supply stores and can be easily machined.

## see also

94
Tools_Vinyl Cutter

121
Insights_Use Soft Boundaries to Partition Open Spaces

# huddle rooms

**A huddle room is a convenient drop-in space for team collaboration.**

The term huddle room gets bandied about quite a bit. For us, they are first-come, first-served rooms for group work.

**Huddle rooms can be used to focus or flare.**
Support both. Create a mix of huddle rooms: some that bias toward flaring, others toward focusing; or outfit rooms flexibly enough to work either way.

**Location: near open spaces.**
Locate the huddle rooms where people will be inclined to drop in (e.g., next to an open office area).

**Quantity: more is better.**
Bias toward having more collaborative spaces than individual spaces.

**Flexibility: let users manipulate it.**
Preserve some flexibility—invariably these spaces will get used for all kinds of activities no matter your initial intent.

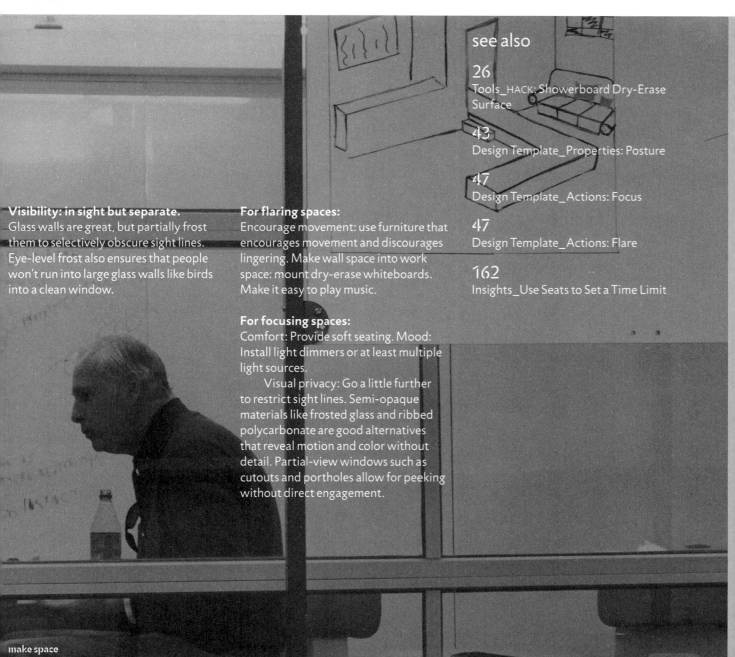

**Visibility: in sight but separate.**
Glass walls are great, but partially frost them to selectively obscure sight lines. Eye-level frost also ensures that people won't run into large glass walls like birds into a clean window.

**For flaring spaces:**
Encourage movement: use furniture that encourages movement and discourages lingering. Make wall space into work space: mount dry-erase whiteboards. Make it easy to play music.

**For focusing spaces:**
Comfort: Provide soft seating. Mood: Install light dimmers or at least multiple light sources.

Visual privacy: Go a little further to restrict sight lines. Semi-opaque materials like frosted glass and ribbed polycarbonate are good alternatives that reveal motion and color without detail. Partial-view windows such as cutouts and portholes allow for peeking without direct engagement.

see also

26
Tools_HACK: Showerboard Dry-Erase Surface

43
Design Template_Properties: Posture

47
Design Template_Actions: Focus

47
Design Template_Actions: Flare

162
Insights_Use Seats to Set a Time Limit

# Make Your Partner Look Good.

**Simple rules, big impact.**
Theatrical improv* works largely because of collective agreement on a few simple rules. One such rule is "make your partner look good." Taken to heart, it makes improv work because everyone is in tune with and supporting each other. Athletes who participate in team sports know the value of this—a good assist is worth more than a risky shot. The same is true for collaboration.

**"Yes, and . . ."**
Listen & accept what others are saying and use their ideas as springboards to build new ones. Pretty soon you will collectively land on a great concept and it will be completely unclear whose idea you are working on. This is an advantage: everyone is now invested.

*Check out Keith Johnstone's book, Impro: Improvisation and the Theatre (Routledge, 1987).

## see also

51
Design Template_Attitudes: Collaborate across Boundaries

# Make Thinking Tangible

**More and more, ideas are coming from the bottom up. All-inclusive expertise and spaces that solidify hierarchies are no longer apt fits for many dynamic domains.**

**Media theorist and futurist Paul Saffo suggests that the United States shifted from a consumer economy to a creator culture in 2008.*** Regardless of when it happened, the world does feel flipped in this age of effortless distribution and a resurgence of do-it-yourself participation.

**Fluid intelligence & tangible thinking.** Neuroscience journalist Jonah Lehrer says intelligence has two parts: crystallized intelligence describing domain knowledge and fluid intelligence as the ability to identify patterns and solve problems.† Amid shifting and burgeoning contexts, leaders and teachers need to be able to embrace both types of intelligence, but spaces need to be reconsidered to support more fluid types of thinking.
    A key to effective leading amidst this creator culture is the ability to uncover, diagnose, synthesize, and respond to collective understanding as

it emerges and evolves. Methods for making thinking "tangible" so it can be touched, stretched, understood, and acted upon, are critical to propel this fluid intelligence.

**Tangible thinking spaces support:**

**Quick visualization.**
Think vertical, writable surfaces and small-scale projection.

**Behavior modeling.**
Get teachers & students and leaders & followers working in the same space, with work visible to each other.

**Making, sharing, and feedback.**
Shape rooms around prototyping, so ideas can be embodied quickly to share with others.

**Closeness, safety, and human understanding.**
Intimacy and connection are critical in

forming trust and bonds—quiet reflection spaces or postures plus eye-to-eye orientation help.

*Paul Saffo, "Get Ready for a New Economy," http://whatmatters.mckinseydigital.com/internet/get-ready-for-a-new-economic-era, February 26, 2009.
†Jonah Lehrer, "A Simple Exercise to Boost IQ," www.wired.com/wiredscience/frontal-cortex, June 11, 2011.

## see also

**22**
Insights_Context Is Content

**51**
Design Template_Attitudes

**88**
Insights_Make a Soundtrack

new space. Others will leverage this momentum.

**Loosen your grip.**
Even better than rewarding people with a desirable space is simply encouraging people to alter the space themselves. Provide mini-budgets for self-motivated space design experiments. The more experiments that pop up, the more the space will bloom.

**Make a gradual shift.**
Make little changes first. Then start radical experiments in targeted areas and expand them as they gain steam.

## see also

# Use Space to Nudge Culture, Not to Shove It.

**We make space and space makes us.**
This theme is woven throughout this book. Space has the capacity to change culture, but there is a limit.

**Design a space that enlivens and pushes but still fits your culture.**
An elegant gown can transform a fashion runway, but it's no good for work in a wood shop. The same principle applies to designing a space.

**Think of space as a nudge, not a catapult.**
If your community's cultural norms don't encourage visualization, you might find that your vision of a colorful, collaborative playground with expanses of whiteboard ends up feeling more like a vacant parking lot in a northern tundra.

**Work on your culture and your space at the same time.**
Encourage and reward behaviors as well as provide for their support.

**Start where it's happening.**
Develop the space around your people. Reward an exemplary team with a great

# Beware of Whiz-Bang!

**The simple solution lasts longer, is always easier to build and iterate, and is usually less esoteric and more adaptable.**

Innovation is all about the new, the possible. We love novel solutions. Articulating arms, convertible furniture, and digitally augmented work surfaces are cool, exciting, and enticing. Given equivalent (or nearly equivalent) performance, the more elegant solution is the one that has the fewest moving parts. So suggests Ockham,* and so say we, sometimes.

Whiz-bang is a balance. Perhaps a highly specialized and fantastically elaborate device is exactly what you need for a particular application (e.g., a linear particle accelerator), and you'll have an individual to run & maintain that system, safely out of reach of bystanders. Great. When you are designing a utility that will be used and manipulated by many (e.g., airplane seats), focus your attention only on the details that transform the ordinary into the extraordinary and on the

mechanisms that can fail and still allow basic functionality. Keep this balance in mind particularly when you build your own things from scratch.

*Try to track down Ockham's pamphlet on the matter. It's tricky. Wikipedia says that Ockham didn't originate the concept, he only popularized it by publicly discussing it. Earlier philosophers (Maimonides, John Duns Scotus, and Aristotle) planted the seeds—a common, if not productive, phenomenon in the history of design (http://en.wikipedia.org/wiki/Occam's_razor).

see also

**96**
Insights_Make Technology Radically Accessible, But Don't Use It Often

**248**
Insights_The Escalator Test

**The zany drains of Kunsthofpassage in Dresden, Germany.**

Transcend the endless
banks of fluorescent tubes
with incandescent bulbs.*

We are in favor of mindfully using resources. Fluorescent tubes perform better than incandescent bulbs in terms of light created versus energy used. Nevertheless, the little fire on the filament is still unparalleled in terms of the warm glow that it creates. Baking cookies & eating them is an entirely different experience from purchasing them from someone for consumption: perhaps baking cookies yourself is less efficient than buying them, but it is representative of a whole experience. So, for what it is worth, we confidently encourage the use of incandescent bulbs in the context of mindfully designed experiences. Use them sparingly, and place them close to people for the biggest impact.

**Incandescence aside, the key is to use several points of warm light.** Several little points of light give a homey, relaxed feel to a space, as opposed to the universal glare of conventional office lighting. However, it's tricky when you need to turn off all the lamps sprinkled throughout your space, since most are individually switched. One way around this is to wire a wall switch that turns multiple outlets off and on. Creatively routing, wrapping, and hiding lamp cords so that they can be grouped on outlet strips can also be worth the effort.

# incandescents
# and dimmers

1.
Buy lightbulb.

2.
Screw bulb into
lamp socket.

**Swap standard light switches for dimmers as soon as you move in.**
A little light tweak can have an incredible impact: you can shift the mood of a space from bright & lively to cool & collected. That restaurant you like, the one with the great vibe? It's got dimmers.

**Important!**
Consult an electrician to discuss the peculiarities of your setup if you've never installed a wall dimmer. Check out YouTube for a short instructional video on installing one (search keywords "installing a dimmer switch"). There are many other tutorials online as well.

* While you can: The U.S. Congress passed the Energy Independence and Security Act in 2007, which may effectively phase out all current incandescent bulbs by 2014.

## sourcing

Your local hardware store or home center will have countless lighting options available. Also investigate specialty lighting sources for commercial applications. Frequently these independent sources offer unique color and wattage selections in both fluorescent & incandescent varieties.

3.
Plug in lamp
& turn it on.

4.
Enjoy.

# Use Seats to Set a Time Limit.

**Pair the comfort of your chairs with the intent of your activity.**
Launch a collaborative session with dynamic seats—for example, the Foam Cubes—and graduate into more comfortable seats for longer activities that might require more sustained attention and singular focus.

**Despite the availability of finely tuned ergonomics, seats that are comfortable for only a short duration can be an advantage.**
Take a cue from the tendencies of toddlers forced to sit still: there is a reason why playgrounds are full of swings and springs rather than ladder-back dining room chairs. Likewise, collaboration among adults often thrives on moving and mingling.

## see also

18
Tools_Foam Cubes

43
Design Template_Properties: Posture

51
Design Template_Attitudes

# Make Space with a Small Team.

**If you want the space to sing, it has to be someone's job to drive the project and play the changes.**
Most organizations simply do not prioritize the continued design of space as a tool for sustained organizational operation. This responsibility falls away with the passing of keys from the construction contractor to the janitorial service.

**Multiple perspectives hone and resolve the design.**
Seek out radically different perspectives and audition your concepts & prototypes with many other people. Collaboration works best when the right perspectives come to bear at the right time: the more disparate the perspectives of the design team, the more likely that gaps will be filled and that novel ideas will emerge.

**When selecting people, focus on relevant experience rather than pedigree.**
For example, we are neither architects nor interior designers, but our combined experiences in filmmaking, structural engineering, design, and education give us the wherewithal to

tackle some pretty esoteric space design projects.

**Small teams make good decisions.**
Decisions have to be made by synthesizing many, often contradictory, threads. We've found this coherency of thought difficult to achieve with large groups. Our norm for the ideal number of decision makers hovers around two to three people.

see also

51
Design Template_Attitudes:
Collaborate across Boundaries

176
Insights_Recognize Your
Emotional Arc during a Project

# theater in the round

**Arrange chairs in a circle or horseshoe shape to inspire an interactive discussion in place of a presentation or lecture.**

Simple but powerful. Lead while sitting in a chair if you want to encourage more discussion. Lead by standing in the center if you need to carry the energy of the room.*

*One caveat: Be aware that if you are "on stage"—that is, at the center of the group—you are being viewed from all angles, front and back.

## start

It's easy. Get rid of rows and arrange chairs in a tight circle. Try it out right away.

## see also

### 32
Situations_Around the Campfire

### 44
Design Template_Properties: Orientation

The shell of the
Nueva I-Lab during
construction.

# Designing Space for Innovation: Learning Inside and Outside the I-Lab

by Alex Ko

In 2007, The Nueva School, a K–8 school in the San Francisco Bay Area, engaged the d.school to design a new innovation space for their campus expansion. Nueva wanted to include design thinking with their emergent curriculum incorporating students' curiosity into free-flowing lessons that were experiential, academic, and cross-disciplinary. The innovation space, which became known as the I-Lab, was meant to support this curriculum in all the ways a classroom filled with desks and chalkboards could not. Oversized wood and foam "Legos" would help students gain empathy in being able to recreate physical experiences. All manner of storage was created to make materials openly available to the students to encourage prototyping as an active part of their work. As one student

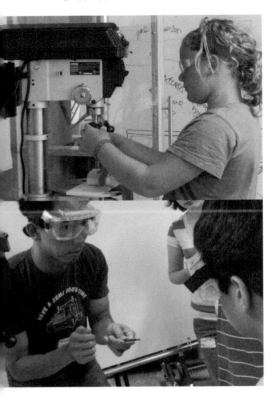

top: A student gets
acquainted with the
drill press.

above: Yusuke
Miyashita
prototypes safety
lessons with
students.

put it, the I-Lab was for doing, "the kind of stuff I can only do when I get home to my garage."

We kicked off the project with a vengeance, deploying a 20-person team on the Nueva campus to observe and dig into the essence of their teaching style. We gutted the d.school for the summer and prototyped the I-Lab at full scale in our own space, using Nueva students and teachers to test everything from new curricula to shop safety, to props for playacting. In three months we learned a lot and thought we came up with a pretty clever & honed concept. The I-Lab opened its doors for a new academic year on time and with a burst of attention.

Four years later, I went back to the I-Lab. Everything was different: our plans for zones specific to the design process were overcome by emergent projects dotting the space, some of the original furniture sat on the sidelines, while new items took their place. As a designer, I found it a bit disconcerting, like making a mushroom pizza, putting it in the oven, then opening the oven to find a piping hot supreme pie instead. Then the kids came in on their lunch hour. They went straight to a mat of artificial turf and started playing a game they had made up based on a lesson about open-water pollution coalescing into an island in the sea. Their goal: Take apart an island made up of plastic bottles, army men, and other oddly shaped items from six feet away using an extended makeshift

arm. Their current prototype was an ingenious contraption that transformed a broomstick, a deflated balloon filled with coffee beans, some string, and a piece of wood into an articulating suction cup. Using the "arm," the students were almost picking up the army man they sought. Kim Saxe, Director of the I-Lab, interjected, "What could you do next?" The responses from the students were instant, varied, and, most important, followed by an emphatic "Let's try it!"

Even to me—an adult and a design professional—the solution was clever and nonobvious. Kim explained, "That's the success of the I-Lab. It's got a 'muck-about' attitude, but it's not about sloppy work." It's about being able to generate and test ideas quickly. In her words, design thinking was "an antidote to perfection . . . and a changed attitude toward failure."

When I left the I-Lab I was still bewildered by how much the space had changed since its conception. By one traditional measure of architecture— timelessness—it seemed we had failed. Several of our original solutions had evolved, and new solutions for new problems had emerged. Several of our predictions had not subsisted. Yet it was hard to ignore that the mission to introduce design thinking to Nueva through the I-Lab seemed so obviously successful based on the profound example I had witnessed coming from ten-year-olds. I now realize that the success of this architecture project was less about the longevity of the lines we drew or the labels we placed on our floor plans. It was about the way the I-Lab continues to serve the teachers and students of Nueva as they prototype and "muck about" with it. Like the proverbial garage, it offers permission to do things you can't do in the tidy confines of the house. The people—and this permission to continuously test and bend the space to their emerging needs—are what will keep the Nueva I-Lab timeless far beyond our interactions with it.

Alex Ko is a product designer with a background in architecture and design. As a d.school Fellow, he was a project leader during the Nueva I-L

Students "mucking around" in the I-Lab

Transformable table with a
work surface that switches
from create to display.

# flip-top table

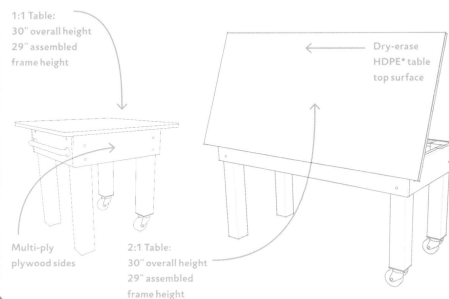

1:1 Table:
30" overall height
29" assembled
frame height

Dry-erase
HDPE® table
top surface

Multi-ply
plywood sides

2:1 Table:
30" overall height
29" assembled
frame height

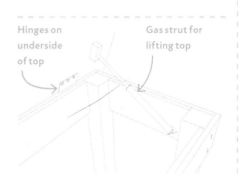

Hinges on
underside
of top

Gas strut for
lifting top

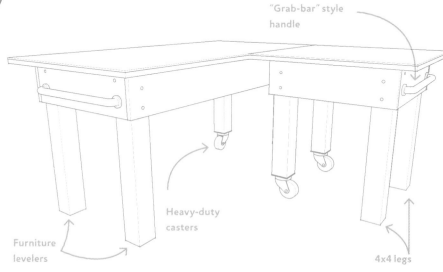

"Grab-bar" style
handle

Heavy-duty
casters

Furniture
levelers

4x4 legs

The Flip-Top Table is a table that accommodates either seated or low-standing-height activity: it can be used for "heads down" horizontal work and, with a flip of the top, vertical presentation or display. This allows a group to work as a tightly knit team, then rapidly shift into sharing mode with a larger group.

The two sizes of Flip-Top Tables can be used independently or in a complementary suite. The basic 2:1 and 1:1 aspect ratios of the tabletops facilitate L-shaped and C-shaped arrangements when multiple tables are assembled; in addition, the tables can be arranged in a regular grid or in long, "buffet-style" configurations to support various activities.

## build instructions

**2:1 Table**
·   30" overall height
·   29" assembled frame height
frame rails (long sides):
·   7" high x 54" long
·   1¹/₂" thick (two ³/₄" plywood pieces)
frame rails (short sides):
·   7" high x 22¹/₂" long
·   1¹/₂" thick (two ³/₄" plywood pieces)
legs (casters):
·   24¹/₂", depending on casters
legs (no casters):
·   28", depending on levelers
tabletop:
·   60" long x 30" wide
·   ³/₄" thick (7-ply plywood)
    or ¹/₈" thick (white HDPE*)

**1:1 Table**
·   30" overall height
·   29" assembled frame height
frame rails (long sides):
·   7" high x 24" long
·   1¹/₂" thick (two ³/₄" plywood pieces)
frame rails (short sides):
·   7" high x 22¹/₂" long
·   1¹/₂" thick (two ³/₄" plywood pieces)
legs (casters):
·   24¹/₂", depending on casters
legs (no casters):
·   28", depending on levelers
tabletop:
·   60" long x 30" wide
·   ³/₄" thick (7-ply plywood)
    or ¹/₈" thick (white HDPE*)

## tips

·   The rails attach to the 4x4 legs via two ¹/₂"-diameter carriage bolts at the top and bottom of each rail. Thus, each leg has two sets of two staggered bolt holes: two from the long rails and two from the short rails.
·   Gas struts are load rated. Depending on the weight of the tabletop, you might need to experiment with a several load ratings. The Flip-Top Tables used two 40-lb. struts.

## sourcing

The Flip-Top Tables were designed & constructed by the d.school for use at the I-Lab facility at Nueva School in Hillsborough, California.

**hardware**
All connecting hardware can be obtained from conventional hardware stores. Gas struts and strut-mounting accessories as well as leg-levelers were sourced from McMaster-Carr. McMaster-Carr (600 N County Line Rd., Elmhurst, IL 60126-2081; 630 600-3600; www.mcmaster.com)

**casters**
Industrial Caster & Wheel Co. (2200 Carden Street, San Leandro, CA 94577; 510 569-8303; www.icwco.com). Reference Stanford d.school red caster in 3" or 5".
California Caster and Hand Truck Company (1400 17th Street, San Francisco, CA 94107; 800 950-8750; www.californiacaster.com)

**HDPE***
Port Plastics (ships regionally) (550 East Trimble Road, San Jose, CA 95131; 408 571-2231; www.portplastics.com)

*High-density polyethylene

## see also

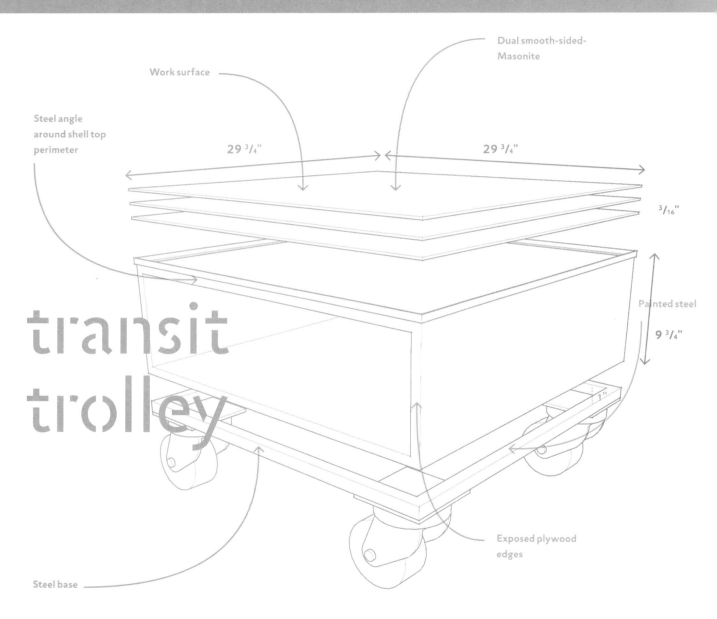

Work surface

Dual smooth-sided-
Masonite

Steel angle
around shell top
perimeter

29 ³/₄"

29 ³/₄"

³/₁₆"

Painted steel

9 ³/₄"

1"

transit
trolley

Exposed plywood
edges

Steel base

Small, mobile surfaces for building, storing, and displaying are critical to a culture of prototyping & testing.

The Transit Trolley is a rock-solid, multipurpose cart with a simple frame for transporting & storing items of all shapes, sizes, and weights. It provides on-the-go support for work in progress.

Multiple sheets of Masonite make the top an expendable work surface: as one layer gets damaged or worn from use, it can be flipped over to expose a fresh surface, or it can be shuffled to expose a new piece of material. A steel lip around the top of the shell contains and aligns the Masonite surfaces.

## start

Furniture dollies make great mobile work surfaces. Attach a plywood top, and go.

## sourcing

### manufacturing
Transit Trolleys were constructed by Stan Heick at HCSI Manufacturing (16890 Church Street, Building 7, Morgan Hill, CA 95037; 408 778-8231; www.hcsidesign.com)

### casters
Industrial Caster & Wheel Co. (2200 Carden Street, San Leandro, CA 94577; 510 569-8303; www.icwco.com). Reference Stanford d.school red caster in 3" or 5".

## see also

### 53
Design Template_Attitudes: Prototype toward a Solution

Oversize "C" clamp handles for pushing

30"

30"

17"

11-ply plywood shell with laminate outer surface

Heavy-duty casters

# storage gallery

**In a nutshell, a storage gallery is a visible display of work in progress, placed prominently for easy discovery.**
This reinvention of storage might be the single most controversial move you can make in the way you work. Actively invite people to look at your secrets: ideas in development, unresolved sketches, and "snapshots" of your thoughts.

**The Storage Gallery has three motivations:**

1. Evidence of activity—signs of work in progress—injects energy into a creative space.
2. Visible work in progress is an invitation for feedback.
3. Artifacts & visuals are vessels for sharing ideas: bottles for messages.

The current Storage Gallery at the d.school consists of an installation of Jacks and Student Boards along the walkway in the main student work studio. Teams store and display their portable work panels, creating a gallery filled with notes, insights, sketches of ideas & prototypes, and diagrams of work in progress. Larger items, such as physical prototypes & artifacts, are displayed in adjacent Storage Towers, so that both rough and elegant prototypes alike remain visible to all who walk by.

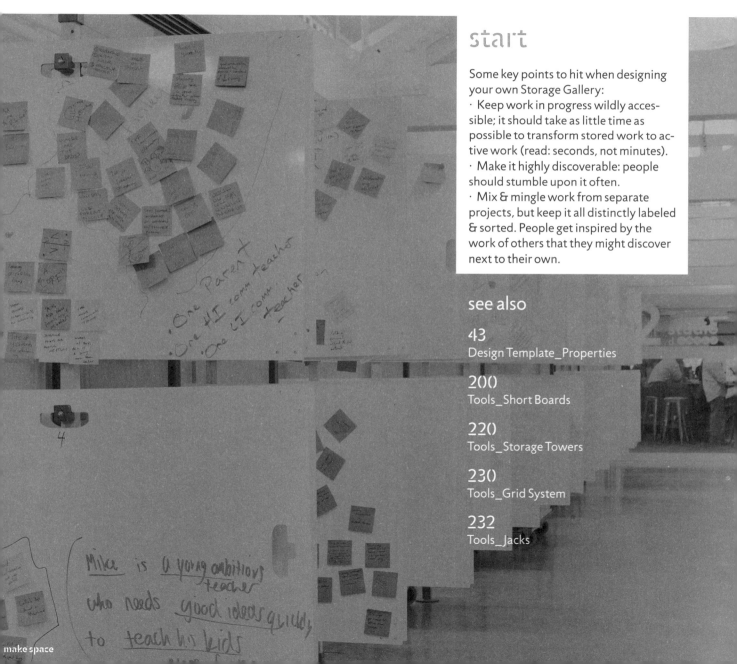

## start

Some key points to hit when designing your own Storage Gallery:

· Keep work in progress wildly accessible; it should take as little time as possible to transform stored work to active work (read: seconds, not minutes).

· Make it highly discoverable: people should stumble upon it often.

· Mix & mingle work from separate projects, but keep it all distinctly labeled & sorted. People get inspired by the work of others that they might discover next to their own.

## see also

# Recognize Your Emotional Arc during a Project.

**This is a note just for you: creative projects have an emotional frequency. Being aware of this can help you successfully navigate the tricky peaks and troughs.**

The arc of a space design process rivals that of any fictional drama. Hopes and dreams hang in the balance. Fear and excitement battle for the upper hand. Egos are invested, and status jockeying abounds. It can be largely frustrating or quite exciting, depending on how you choose to experience it.

As you progress, you will likely encounter the following phenomena. If you know how to recognize them, you can at least reconcile how you are doing with how the project is doing.

**+ A sense of excitement and limitless possibility.** An idea or discovery arrives shiny and new, without the eventual scuff marks inherent in the process of bringing it to fruition. The sense of potential is empowering, yet rarely realistic. It's like buying a Ferrari without yet having found a mechanic to service it. Enjoy this part as it happens, but not so much that you are afraid to let it go.

**– Overwhelming complexity.** As soon as you dig into a space, you'll uncover a seemingly endless pile of emotional and logistical factors simultaneously at play. This is quicksand. Too much thinking here means trouble. When you are in this territory, focus on doing. Get right to prototyping through quick mock-ups and experiences. Acknowledge and categorize new issues as they arise, but prioritize—you'll never be able to resolve all of them. Keep your eyes open for inspiration and direction away from the soup of complexity.

**+ Unifying insights.** These are moments of clarity when you feel you've got it all figured out. They are the siren songs: glorious but potentially derailing. Strive with all your might to get to this point, but diligently question this clarity when you arrive.

**– Complete loss of confidence.** What was I thinking? I can't do this. You can, and in fact, you are doing it. This feeling is mostly useless, although it may signal that you should enlist some help to tackle a specific issue. If so, get the help you need. If your loss of confidence is merely the legacy of some past experience, ignore it by taking new action.

**– The brutal realities of implementation.** Almost everything you do will take longer than you think because there is a lot more to consider than is apparent. You will have to make compromises. Have the strength to stand up for the right things and the wisdom to let go of the meaningless bits. The ability to know how and when to do this often comes from the proof & intuition you'll acquire through prototyping.

**+ Completion.** It's done! Enjoy the sense of accomplishment. You may also experience some postpartum malaise. Fine—that's natural, but don't wallow in it. Do take time to celebrate your accomplishment and reflect on your process. You're never really done anyway; you will likely repeat at least some part of this process someday. Reflection is important to make your next steps more efficient.

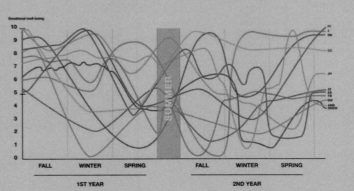

**A plot of the self-described emotional well-being among Stanford graduate design students.**

# Walls vs. Open Space

**Paradox: Walls support collaboration, yet collaborative spaces thrive in openness.**

**Openness is an engine of innovation.**
Openness in the form of visibility and room to move breeds awareness and spawns intersections that keep people inspired and keep projects in tune.

**Walls are terrific display surfaces.**
Walls and vertical surfaces are great for making ideas visible across a group. Visual evidence of work inspires and supports discovery and synthesis.

**Damn.**
This wall/open space conundrum is one of the never-ending challenges of creative space. Thinking of walls as surfaces rather than separators helps inform when, where, and how they can be used. What was once a sliding glass door can be reconsidered as a work surface for capturing & displaying ideas. Sliding and curtain walls, temporary rolling walls, and translucent walls all help solve this equation, as do light-weight but rigid sheet materials such as foamboard coupled with stands (as in the Scoop Stool).

## see also

118
Tools_Scoop Stool

150
Tools_Bulk Sheet Materials

190
Tools_Writable Surfaces Everywhere

# Apply Convention, Defy Convention.

**Use convention when it serves your needs. Blow it up when it doesn't.**

Conventional solutions can work just fine. Don't change them. Do know why you are using them. At the time of this writing, a design convention is to have open kitchens with islands, in both homes and studios. Installing an open-plan, island-centered kitchen in your work space might be the perfect way to support a desired familial gregarious-ness. Simply apply the convention, and your work is done!

Let's say that in your culture long periods of uninterrupted work are beneficial. Maybe an enclosed kitchen

that is isolated from the work space would be less distracting to people who are engrossed in big projects. In this case, defy convention!

Or combine the two: design an open kitchen in an isolated area. Whatever you decide, just be intentional and authentic to your culture.

## see also

66
Insights_Define Your Intent

# Don't Blow the Whole Budget.

see also

**76**
Insights_Leave Room to Evolve

**97**
Insights_Pick Your Spending Spots

**The moment a project is "complete" and people begin to react to their new surroundings, new needs inevitably emerge.**
"Nothing endures but change," said the Greek philosopher Heraclitus some 1,500 years ago. Paradoxically, he's still right.

**Put some money aside for later.**

Sounds easy. It's not. Most annual budgets and grants aren't structured to hold money aside for contingencies. Plan ahead. If you don't have a mattress or floorboards to hide some extra cash, split the money for the project over a couple of budgets as soon as the project begins: one for outfitting the space (the normal retrofitting & furniture/move-in budget) and another budget for iterating and maintaining the space (usually for the following year). Save more than you think you'll need.

# bleacher blocks

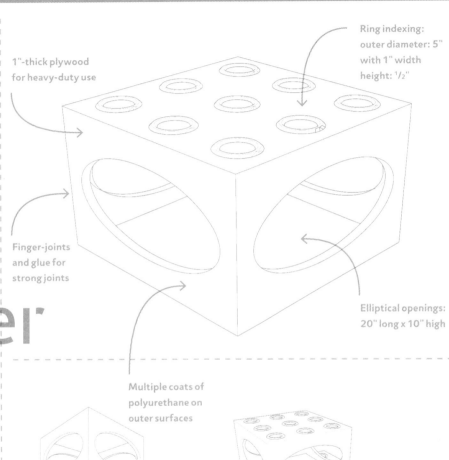

Ring indexing:
outer diameter: 5"
with 1" width
height: $\frac{1}{2}$"

1"-thick plywood
for heavy-duty use

Finger-joints
and glue for
strong joints

Elliptical openings:
20" long x 10" high

Multiple coats of
polyurethane on
outer surfaces

Bleacher Blocks are plywood pieces that link together to create novel platform surfaces for seating, standing, and climbing.

The top and bottom surfaces of each Bleacher Block have ring details to create "positive" and "negative" indexing to align stacked blocks—like human-scale Legos. They adapt to support highly varied activities. Originally intended as building blocks for an impromptu bleacher, the Bleacher Blocks work well as tables, room partitions, storage & shelving units, and infrastructure for immersion prototypes.

## build instructions

**three different shapes:**

· rectangle
· square
· triangle

**rectangle dimensions:**

· height: 18"
· length: 60"
· width: 30"

**square dimensions:**

· height: 18"
· length: 30"
· width: 30"

**triangle (right triangle) dimensions:**

· height: 18"
· short side length: 60"

## start

Cardboard boxes & plastic milk crates can work as early versions of Bleacher Blocks. Setting up an interesting configuration as a default (e.g., a pyramid shape or different patterns at one level) can be a great way to introduce the Bleacher Blocks for use.

## sourcing

Rob Bell at Zomadic, LLC (San Francisco, CA; www.zomadic.com) constructed the Bleacher Blocks.

## see also

**23**
Insights_Design for Primates

# the white room

Booth Blanc—the White Room—in the current d.school building.

## start

Install dry-erase surfaces not just on a single wall but on two adjacent walls and from floor to ceiling. Showerboard is the easiest and cheapest option. Limit seating so that work surfaces get the most attention.

## see also

**26**
Tools_HACK: Showerboard Dry-Erase Surface

**48**
Design Template_Actions: Saturate

**52**
Design Template_Attitudes: Show, Don't Tell

**An immersive experience is one of the quickest ways to transform behavior.**
The White Room concept creates an environment with a singular finish and function that focuses team members on particular activities. Their ideas become the only color that fills the space.

**Why white? It gives you a chance to go all out . . . not halfway.**
Install showerboard, or another dry-erase surface, from floor to ceiling. This unlikely availability of surface provokes teams to be visual & prolific. People can easily fill a page: the intent with the White Room is to make an immersive & tactile page at the scale of a room.

**Key considerations for creating your White Room:**

**Boundless writable surfaces.**
Install it everywhere. Seriously. An advantage of using showerboard is that you can easily cut it to fit in almost any location. Cover every nook & cranny—it's worth the effort.

**Limited furniture.**
Don't cram the space full of places to sit, since the White Room is intended to be an active space. Use casual, upright seating like stools to promote active postures. If you want, add a couch for softness.

**Small space.**
The stark surfaces pair well with tight quarters. If the space is too big, the impact of the white becomes apocalyptic. As a reference point, the d.school has had great success with White Rooms sized at 10' x 14' and even smaller at 8' x 10'.

# Horizontal Surfaces Attract Clutter.

This is an earth-shattering bulletin. Strangely, though, for something that is so intuitive to many, it is an often-ignored phenomenon that routinely impacts the way people create. Horizontal surfaces in a creative culture are like flypaper that collects remnants of false starts and exploratory trajectories, not to mention empty cups.

What can you do about it? Keep horizontal spaces to a minimum and place them prominently to serve active work rather than dormant piles. Use adjacent & accessible shelves to handle piles & tools. Force regular or occasional cleanup through room resets or "spring cleanings."

## see also

# Technology in Your Pocket

**The best technology can often be found in your pocket.**
By literally leaving the technology in the hands of your community, you can develop a more useful and flexible space. Being tech-savvy with a cutting-edge environment is not necessarily about installing the latest of everything but supporting the technology that people instinctively use. New technologies often have better traction from a bottom-up, as opposed to a top-down, approach as people share their personal techniques through word of mouth.

**Instead of oversolving problems with elaborate electronic solutions, act like a tech outfitter.**
People are comfortable with their smart phones, laptops, & tablets—they serve as capture devices, Web browsers, communication devices, and everything else. These existing tools have the advantage of familiarity, ubiquity, and strong communities of tech support. Oftentimes, their use requires minor technical work-arounds (e.g., people e-mailing pictures to themselves), but the flexibility of leveraging personal devices almost always beats out investing in an expensive machine that can solve the problem but is not used because it is unfamiliar or unapproachable.

see also

96
Insights_Make Technology Radically Accessible, But Don't Use It Often

# Building a Runway for Entrepreneurs

## by Corey Ford

When I joined the foundational team at Innovation Endeavors—an early-stage venture capital firm backed by Google's executive chairman, Eric Schmidt—my challenge was to build a program for entrepreneurs to create and launch disruptive ventures from scratch. The Runway Program would be a pre-team, pre-idea venture creation incubator that would help aspiring entrepreneurs form multidisciplinary teams and then support them through a structured six-month process to launch a company based on meeting a deep, unmet need. As my colleague, Celestine Johnson, and I began this space project, we realized the trick was to be clear on what key activities, mindsets, and cultural values we wanted to promote, and then understand how they could be manifested in a specific space solution. A few key principles drove our decisions:

**Embrace imperfection.**
In realizing this culture of companies, we embraced investigation, experimentation, and iteration when it came to building out the space, and we ask the same of our teams. We knew that "getting it right" is more about evolving to suit needs than nailing it on the first try. We decided never to make a decision that would "pour the space in concrete."

left:
Ideas wrap a
column in the center
of the space.

right:
The main
space where
entrepreneurial
teams drop in to
learn & work.

top:
A team from the
Runway Program at
work in the space.

bottom:
2x4 table
construction and
concrete flooring
contribute to a
sense of an active
atmosphere.

When we first invited an architect to help us, the idea of not getting it right from the start was completely foreign to him. He was used to clients that expected him to deliver "perfection." So we had to stick to our principles and constantly reinforce the message that imperfection was okay. Once he trusted us, he ran with it. Soon, he was suggesting that we build our own desks with two-by-fours. The idea of a Peg-Board wall with modular components was sparked. We were now solidly on our way to realizing the potential in imperfection.

**Make the default state high energy, lean forward, and collaborative.**
Buzz is important to us. We thought about where our previous office experiences had fallen short in that regard. Most spaces communicated that work meant sitting at your desk typing on a computer. We called this state "the potted plant." We love our gardens, but we're looking for a zoo. We also hypothesized that the default state of "potted plant" was ubiquitous, so we needed to embrace an active state in no uncertain terms. What did that mean for us? Standing-height desks and chairs are the norm throughout the office. We even preset the chairs with straight backs so they're not "too comfortable." Computers are laptops, and storage is decoupled from the desks to further encourage changes in seating.

**Celebrate getting out into the world.**
Finally, we thought that for our entrepreneurs to be successful they needed to spend at least half of their time out of the building interacting with users and experts to discover their needs and validate their solutions. How could we reinforce that inside the space? We created displays on wheels that were easily set and reset so that teams could broadcast their work in a visually persistent way. This encouraged active turnover in response to new work. Like a gym where members rotate in and out at different hours, we can increase our utilization of the space through our "venture out and drop back in" culture. We can invite even more entrepreneurs to the table and keep the space consistently buzzing even when some are out in the field.

As we move forward with our first iteration, I would be lying if I said this project has been comfortable and easy. Space design takes courage. We strive to balance chaos and concentration, imperfection and professionalism. We're cultivating an eagerness for feedback and simultaneously developing a thick skin that's necessary for making unpopular—albeit well-intended—decisions aimed at changing cultural values. It's tricky, but our intentional imperfection allows us room to learn and change as we move to address the same deep needs we ask of our entrepreneurs. It's worth it.

Corey Ford is Director of Innovation Endeavors' Runway program. He has a professional background in documentary film production and an educational background in business and in journalism. Corey was a d.school Fellow from 2008 to 2009.

Dry-erase surfaces support instantaneous innovation.

Corrugated polycarbonate is a lightweight option for large panels—try $^5/_8$" thickness for large panels & $^1/_4$" for small panels.

Showerboard can be cut into almost any shape for a custom fit or fun application.

writable surfaces everywhere

Install dry-erase surfaces all over the place to create opportunities for capturing serendipitous sketches and outbreaking brainstorms.

### Get creative about what you use for a dry-erase surface.

Corporate-style dry-erase surfaces are often conventional and costly. Try using alternative materials in various shapes & configurations to inspire your audience.

### Most smooth, nonporous materials work well as dry-erase surfaces. Pick a material to match the look and feel of your space.

Readily available options such as acrylic, polycarbonate, showerboard, painted steel, and glass can constitute exciting alternatives to boring board-room boards.

Acrylic and polycarbonate come in transparent and translucent forms. These are great options when glass is too heavy or expensive. Both acrylic and polycarbonate can be cut to fit into interesting nooks & crannies or just cut into interesting shapes. Predrill holes into your sheet materials and mount them to walls with attractive screws & hardware. Run them floor to ceiling or for the full length of a wall without framing the edges to provide a sense of unlimited space for scribing.

### Don't limit yourself to the walls!

Showerboard is easily cut and shaped with basic woodworking tools. Transform a tabletop or a counter by gluing or screwing down some showerboard. Completely cover a standing-height bar table for a unique place to work & doodle.

## tip

· When you transform a table, go the extra step and use a router to round over all the edges so that everything is comfortable to touch.

## sourcing

Acrylic and polycarbonate materials are available in many varieties (dimensions, colors, configurations).

**polycarbonate/acrylic**
Port Plastics (550 East Trimble Road, San Jose, CA 95131; 408 571-2231; www.portplastics.com) ships regionally.
TAP Plastics (154 South Van Ness, San Francisco, CA 94103; 800 246-5055; www.tapplastics .com) has many western U.S. locations.

**showerboard**
Showerboard is available at most home centers and local lumber suppliers.
Pine Cone Lumber (895 East Evelyn Avenue, Sunnyvale, CA 94086; 408 736-5491; www.pineconelumber.com). Reference "solid white tileboard" or "showerboard."

## start

Buy a few 4' x 8' sheets of showerboard at a home center and mount them on any wall. Done! Huge, instant writing surfaces at a fraction of the cost of conventional office-style boards.

We borrowed this next idea from our friends at the Stanford Center for Design Research. Have a sealed window? Use the glass as a writing surface. Alternate option: Install a sheet of acrylic over the window casing to create a large, see-through surface.

## see also

Keep your brand thriving
with simple analog
dynamic displays.

# simple
# dynamic ID
# wall displays

**Signal that you are a dynamic, human-centered organization:** Make your identity wall changeable on the fly and identify your space by celebrating the people within it. Use individual photo "tiles" or larger changeable panels in lieu of fixed signage and logos.

**Feature people to communicate your current culture.**
Posting recent photographs front and center forges a simple and immediate connection with everyone who enters your space. Alternatively, highlight visiting teachers & special guests with a photo and a note to announce their presence to all who enter.

## build instructions

**option 1:**
**photo tiles**

Make simple photo tiles by spray-adhering printed photos to a yardstick, foamboard, or sheet magnets. Shift and shuffle photo tiles to create an engaging installation.

Use a nice-looking magnetic mounting surface such as sheet metal, magnetic chalkboard, or lattice-cut steel.

Mount photos with magnets or binder clips. Easy-to-grab magnets should be at least $^1/_2$" tall. Strong magnets should hold at least 2 lb.

Durable mounting encourages shuffling of the photos.
· Galvanized steel is magnetic; stainless may not be.
· Carefully predrill screw pilot holes so you don't pucker the material with the screws.
· Pay attention to the look of the screw head: it will be visible.

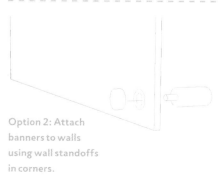

Option 2: Attach banners to walls using wall standoffs in corners.

**option 2:**
**dynamic panels**

Identify your ID wall or the wall you want to brand, and install "panel standoffs" to hold all types of banners: paper, fabric, plastic, glass, etc. Space standoffs strategically to accommodate common banner sizes.

Plot, print, cut, or source your panels.

Install grommets on the panels and align them with the standoff spacings.

Alternative: Use wire and clips.

## tips

· Practice restraint, or get a graphic designer involved in creating visual layouts.
· Check with suppliers or materials vendors to get a list of conventional sizes before you place the pegs (e.g., common fabric width, foamboard width, plotter width).
· Get a grommet kit to create panel-mounting holes in your workplace.

## sourcing

**magnets**
One online source offering a wide variety of shapes and sizes is K&J Magnets (888 746-7556; www.kjmagnetics.com).

## start

Mount a big (at least 2' x 4') piece of sheet metal to the wall in a prominent location. Have the metal cut in an interesting aspect ratio (width-to-height relationship)—e.g., a long and narrow strip 8' x 2'. Get too many magnets (100). Take candid digital photos of everyone, using the same background in each. Print the photos and use magnets to mount and re-arrange them on the sheet metal.

**sheet metal**
Local hardware and home centers have sheet metal varieties. The d.school sources elaborate perforated metal at McNichols (nationwide locations). In the San Francisco Bay Area: 19226 Cabot Blvd., Hayward, CA 94545-1143; 877 884-4653; www.mcnichols.com).

**panel standoff**
Find a large selection of standoffs and accompanying hardware at McMaster-Carr (600 N County Line Rd., Elmhurst, IL 60126; 630 600-3600; www.mcmaster.com).

Many options exist for creating fabric banners from digital graphics (for example). The d.school ID banners were printed by CanvasPop (2753 Broadway Suite 374, New York, NY 10025; 866 619-9574; www.canvaspop.com).

open office
seating

make space

## start

With your community, identify a few working styles and create corresponding seating configurations in response to those themes. Assign to each one a title that suggests a particular behavior. Determine a short duration for trying out each style, then regroup and make changes.

## see also

**196**
Insights_The Open Office Floor Plan Has a Shadow

**224**
Situations_The Coffee Shop

**An open office, free from traditional walls, is not exempt from the personal and professional motivations behind those walls.**
Breaking down conventions by breaking down walls requires careful consideration of how, where, and why people sit when they work. A few strategic approaches can set successful precedents in evolving an open office community.

**Even "heads down" work rarely takes place continuously in one spot. And it shouldn't.**
People get up to eat, walk around, chat, and use tools. Now that laptops are the norm, it's easy to imagine getting office work done in a lounge chair. This is a productive and healthy advantage in an open office, where people can change posture and intersect with folks they wouldn't ordinarily encounter.

**General admission: supply more seats than people.**
Give everyone a desk and also provide secondary drop-in seating. Supply about 30 percent more seating than the number of people you have to keep things fluid.

**Create neighborhoods, each with its own metaphor.**
The Picnic Table: a long, open table, where anyone can stop by. The Hotel Lobby: big lounge-worthy couches with dimly lit surroundings. The Diner: high-backed booth seating with a table in the middle.

**Position each neighborhood thoughtfully.**
Lounge seating is a convenient buffer between an entrance and a work space; folks can focus on work while engaging in the action. The Picnic Table works well near the kitchen. A Library might be positioned away from visitor traffic and noise.

# The Open Office Floor Plan Has a Shadow.

**"Everyone carries a shadow, and the less it is embodied in the individual's conscious life, the blacker and denser it is." —Carl Gustav Jung**

**The shadow side of an overly collaborative space is a shunning of collaboration.**

**Collaboration is partly personal.**
This book is primarily about collaborative spaces, not the individual spaces that also need to be in place to support creative work. But personal spaces need to be in place in even the most collaborative space. As Rudyard Kipling explains in The Second Jungle Book, "For the strength of the pack is the wolf, and the strength of the wolf is the pack." The success of a collaborative effort is inextricably linked to the success of the individual.

People will find ways to service their needs. If you provide no respite from collaborating, no alternative other than being social, people will seek shelter elsewhere and your fabulous space will remain empty. Darkening this shadow is the loss of a sense of belonging that previously was a benefit of having an owned personal space. Whew! Heavy.

**The takeaway: Split your time and effort between curating and cultivating.**
Curate by providing for the individual with personal space, quiet space, private space, and a bevy of amenities. Over-the-top finishing touches and special surprises, such as custom lounges & hip, family-style eating areas tend to increase feelings of pride and belonging. No need to be ridiculously lavish in your spending, but providing a bit of TLC is worth the expenditure.

Cultivate by activating and encouraging your community to shape itself with hacks, modifications, and embellishments. This might mean personal artifacts stacked on display here and there or potted plants finding their way into the scene. An open office can be a platform responsive to change rather than a single, fixed solution.

*Carl Gustav Jung, Psychology and Religion: West and East, CW 11, 1938, p. 131 Princeton.

## see also

# The Responsibility-Adjustability Slide Rule

**The more responsible users are for a space, the more adjustable the space can be.**
There are plenty of exceptions to this axiom, but it is a good rule of thumb for gut-checking your intent & vision with the realities of implementation.

**Room configurations need not be simple, but they should be considered in the context of likely users.**
If you are thinking about designing a multifunction space that will host activities planned and executed by all different kinds of people, you should consider how those people might engage it. Think about seeing a movie in a theater versus at an amphitheater in the park. The theater is focused on creating a curated experience in a high-turnover scenario where the audience has little control. In the park, on the other hand, a hillside is a different platform for a once-in-a-while experience that the audience members craft with their own blankets, chairs, and food. Same movie, different relationships.

## see also

**20**
Situations_Instant/Shared Studio

**30**
Insights_Start with What You Have

# Bold Is Better than Bland.

**Contrast is perhaps the greatest design tool.**

It emphasizes or deemphasizes via difference.

It is a full moon in a night sky.

It was Arnold Schoenberg in 1923 and the Ramones in 1976.

It is the difference between a meeting in which you actually do something and most any office meeting.

**Don't be afraid to overdo it a little bit. Memorable environments are memorable because they are out of the ordinary.**

While striking, however, extremes in themselves have little staying power without a solid expression of meaning and purpose. Spaces that emphasize and embody core values are the most compelling because of their transparent authenticity.

Two literally transparent examples are I. M. Pei's crystal pyramid facade at the front of the Louvre in Paris and the glass cube over the underground Apple Store on 5th Avenue in New York. Both structures are unlikely in their use of glass as walls, and, more important, they are almost obscenely different from the surrounding structures. Yet both of them amplify the ethos of their respective organizations: risky and worth it.

## see also

**66**
Insights_Define Your Intent

**134**
Insights_Design Strong Points & Counterpoints

**The Apple Store entrance above ground on 5th Avenue in Manhattan.**

# Powers of Ten

**When observing & designing a space, consider it in multiple scales, from the level of the individuals' hands to the scope of an entire neighborhood.**

In 1968, the husband-and-wife design team Charles and Ray Eames created Powers of Ten,* a seminal film that focuses first on a rather mundane event, a picnic in the park. The action unfolds by sequentially reframing the setting by a visual order of magnitude, a "power of ten." One moment the picnickers are in clear sight, and the next they are diminished, appearing unrecognizably small, as the scene reveals the Earth in the context of the cosmos. The Eameses then reverse the action, traveling back to the picnickers and focusing the composition orders of magnitude smaller—at the molecular level.

The film is so stunning not because of any drama but because it considers a subject—the picnic—at a range of scales, that is, in widely divergent contexts. This suggests a useful tool for understanding and responding to contexts for the purpose of design.

To put it simply, when designing for a space examine each aspect of the situation from different levels of granularity. Let's say you are observing a meeting in which a heated argument is taking place. Observe how the individual participants are experiencing the argument (revealed by cues such as posture and orientation toward each other). Then zoom out: how does the acoustics of the room support the ability to argue? What are the larger contexts and cultures that have influenced the way people are behaving? Use this strategy to push yourself to become engaged with the space in new ways and to reveal new insights.

*Powers of Ten is available for viewing at the Eames Foundation website: www.powersoften .com. The film is an adaptation of Kees Boeke's book, Cosmic View: The Universe in 40 Jumps (J. Day, 1957). This is an excellent work that is worth pursuing.

## see also

36
Insights_Follow the Hacks: Innovation Is Everywhere

249
Insights_It's about People

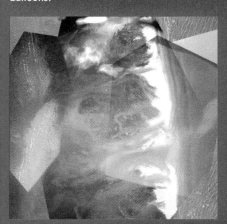

**DIY aerial documentation of the 2010 Gulf of Mexico oil spill; created using a camera strapped to balloons.**

Lightweight, portable panels for storing and displaying persistent project notes, pictures, and plans.

short boards

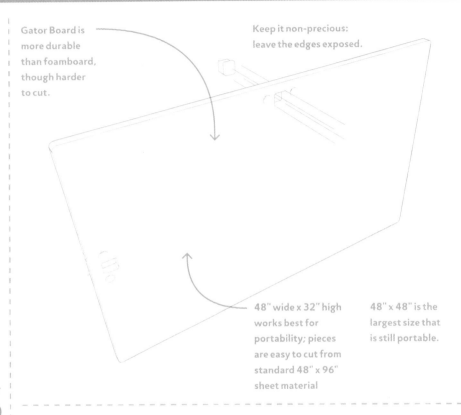

Gator Board is more durable than foamboard, though harder to cut.

Keep it non-precious: leave the edges exposed.

48" wide x 32" high works best for portability; pieces are easy to cut from standard 48" x 96" sheet material

48" x 48" is the largest size that is still portable.

One or both sides can be coated with dry-erase paint, adhesive dry-erase sheets, or showerboard.

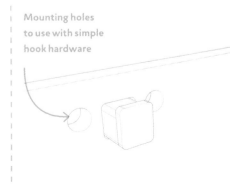

Mounting holes to use with simple hook hardware

Short Boards work great with Post-its and adhered photographs. Information can be rearranged and displayed as the nature of the work changes. Portable size enables you to set up instant individual and team work spaces. Mounting hardware allows for storage and display in multiple locations.

Short Boards respond to the challenge of providing as much work space to as many people as possible. Teams use Short Boards to capture & manipulate information during active work and then store & display the work when they take a break. Instead of relying on a "Do Not Erase" note over critical information, teams can reliably keep their information on Short Boards that can be set up and used anywhere.

Short Boards are meant to be displayed. Cut circular mounting holes using a 2" to 3" hole-cutting bit and a drill. These holes double as handles for carrying. Installing simple hardware hooks or pegs around your space creates storage spots as well as potential team spaces.

## sourcing

The d.school currently uses Short Boards with a configuration developed in collaboration with Steelcase. The boards feature dual-sided dry-erase surfaces and holes that work in conjunction with custom mounting pegs.

**foamboard**
Arch Supplies (99 Missouri Street, San Francisco, CA 94107; 415 433-2724; www.archsupplies.com)

**foamboard / gator board**
ULINE Shipping Supply Specialists (800 958-5463; www.uline.com)

**mounting hardware**
The d.school uses custom-made mounting pegs designed to allow one peg per board mounting. Standard "L"-hook hardware is readily available at any hardware store. These hooks hold many Short Boards.
McMaster-Carr (600 North County Line Road; Elmhurst, IL 60126; 630 600-3600; www.mcmaster.com)

## start

Buy & cut foamboard to size. Start with Short Boards that are 48" x 32" and get 3 boards from a 4' x 8' sheet with no waste. Cut a stack of them and mount them in prominent places. Install hooks in multiple locations to encourage use in those locations. Transform a hallway by installing hooks & Short Boards.

## see also

20
Situations_Instant / Shared Studio

240
Tools_Connectors

describes it as a place to pause or lean for a brief encounter. A stool next to a bar can be a perch, but so can the back of a chair or the arm of a couch.

Create deliberate perches to promote an active culture. Stepping away from a stool requires a lot less energy than climbing out from the low, soft seat of a couch. In dynamic spaces, deliberate perches are a welcome feature—they provide a moment of rest in a way that allows people to easily flow in and out of the action. Deliberately small tables complement the situation: like cocktail tables, they provide enough space to prop up little items but not enough to spread out a four-course meal.

## see also

# Provide Quick Perches in Active Spaces.

A "perch" is a well-known term in design and furniture industry lingo. Steelcase R&D guru Frank Graziano aptly

# Patina Gives Permission.

**When designing a creative environment, default to "studio" or "workshop," not "office."**

If you are actually intending to create a studio, you'll have one. If your intent was to create a conference room, you'll end up with a cool conference room, unlike any other.

**The best creative spaces are highly resolved (thoughtful), but not highly refined (precious).**
Walk into even the most organized and refined of art studios and you will have evidence of the creative process—paint on a concrete floor, holes in the walls, and cut marks on tabletops. This is desirable; it means work is happening. Creativity is often a messy affair even if your work space has never seen and will never see a tube of paint—notice your piles of paper, open pens, and various food utensils.

**Use non-precious materials in active/ making spaces.**
Use surfaces that can stand up to a little wear and tear. This signals that it is okay to open up and get a bit dirty while exploring options. Using non-precious, lightly finished surfaces lessens concern about the furnishings and lets the mind focus on the task at hand. Think butcher-block table in an active kitchen.

**Amid the chaos, creative spaces are carefully considered and often well organized.**
Time spent searching for tools and incessantly rearranging furniture is not time well spent.

## see also

37
Insights_Expose Raw Materials

244
Insights_Provide Permission, Say "Yes," Mostly

# meeting place

**Reframe the conference room as a place to meet & mingle.**
Conventional conference rooms are all about status and sides: long rooms & long tables put special emphasis on the heads of the table. Also, sitting face-to-face forces a face-off. Arthur had something going with the Round Table.

**Create a comfortable, human space in which people can come together.**
Call it what you like, but a conference room gets used for a whole lot more than conferences. "Meeting" has malleable meanings: it can refer to anything from a perfunctory project check-in to an intimate conversation. Create a space that can adapt to this diversity of situations. Although it has taken on a somewhat negative connotation—who likes work meetings?—the word itself describes the most human of engagements: meet•ing (noun): a coming together of two or more people.*

**The facets of a good meeting place:**

**Comfort.**
The space should feel good (literally & figuratively): physically comfortable & visually calm. This is a place to invest in some nice furniture and fixtures—but think "home," not "office."

**Reconfigurability.**
First, make sure you can get the table out of the way when you need to by putting it on casters or investing in a collapsible table. Create at least one scenario that supports more intimate conversations—for example, soft cushions that you can arrange on the floor.

**Acoustic privacy.**
If you have a lot of open-plan spaces, this is especially important. It's good to have the option for private conversations as needed.

**Variable visibility.**
A little visibility is a nice feature—it permits a glimpse of the activity in the room and prevents people from having to knock at the door to see who's inside. However, at times it is important for the room's occupants to feel secure and free from view—frosted glass does the trick.

**Big enough to hold 8 to 12 people, but intimate enough for 2 to share.**
A room between 12' x 12' and 15' x 20' works well. That's big. Use dark and/or warm colors & soft surfaces (wallpaper is pleasingly disarming) to make the space feel a little more intimate.

**Square if you can.**
The long & skinny conference room matches the long conference tables and reinforces status relationships by making it hard to move around.

**Limit the duration of use.**
Allow time enough to sync up, no more. Use project rooms for extended meetings.

**Multiple lighting options.**
It's convenient to be able to switch between a high-key, bright work mode (e.g., fluorescent lighting) and a quiet, spot-lit, chatting ambience (e.g., using incandescent floor or hanging lamps).

**Lots of space to visualize.**
Keep the projector. Burn the little flip-chart. Add wall-scale writing surfaces (e.g., floor-to-ceiling whiteboards).

*"meeting," Apple Dictionary. 2011.

## start

Grab a conference room. Lose the table. Repaint the walls. Drop in some soft furniture.

## see also

**44**
Design Template_Properties: Orientation

**45**
Design Template_Properties: Ambience

**128**
Tools_HACK: See-Through Walls

**160**
Tools_HACK: Incandescents and Dimmers

# Experimental Kitchen

## by Ben Roche

make space

# Space Studies_Experimental Kitchen

Moto is a restaurant focused on pushing the envelope not just in culinary ideas but in how a fine dining restaurant is set up, organized, and run—successfully, we hope. We were one of the first restaurants in the United States to implement a rotation system of front and back of house, meaning that all servers (or waiters) are chefs, but not all chefs are servers . . . not yet. A calm, cool, smoothly running dining room is a different universe from a hot, noisy kitchen on a busy night. Somehow we collectively manage to exist effectively in both worlds from one day to the next.

### Shift modes: use the same space in different ways

In a professional kitchen, space is very limited. Chefs are forced to be creative when organizing, maintaining, and utilizing everything around them. At Moto, it's even more complex, as the space changes functions every day at around five o'clock. The kitchen staff spends the first half of the day doing prep work. During this time, there are boxes of ingredients, notebooks, cutting boards, immersion circulators, liquid nitrogen dewars, etc. all laid out on the tables. Dinner service starts at five, at which point the tabletops are cleared and lined with stacks of polished plates and any special tools or mise en place that will be used frequently for plating.

### Experiment with a clean slate

Experimentation and new dish happen during the day while prep and other

top left:
Experimenting with liquid nitrogen.

above:
Containing elemental ingredients.

# Space Studies_Experimental Kitchen

projects are under way. Any time between steps (when something is cooking or dehydrating or gelling) is spent working on other projects. One improbable key to productive experimentation is extreme organization. When a tool or ingredient or anything else is out of place, it's distracting. This gets amplified when time is limited and we chefs are hastily dodging each other.

### The "rage cage": keep everything within arm's reach

The most important aspect of a chef's personal space in the kitchen is accessibility. If it takes an extra step to grab something, you may find yourself going down when it gets really busy. In my corner of the kitchen I'm surrounded by my "rage cage"—a network of work surfaces, tools, and equipment meticulously arranged so that everything I need is a step, a reach, a sweet spin-move, or a quick pivot away. The goal is to almost literally not have to move from one central spot while executing between seven and ten completely different dishes. This can be planned to a certain point, but there is obviously quite a lot of trial and error, so flexibility is important in not getting too attached to a particular setup.

### Surround yourself with good humor
On the side of a large refrigerator that faces me—not visitors—I have an assortment of art and objects that helps keep me grounded and sane while

I'm working: a napkin drawing I did of a crazed-looking former co-worker, a giant hand made out of masking tape and Sharpie giving the middle finger; cutouts of logos from boxes of ingredients that I think are funny, little statues of random people, and a bike horn—the kind that you honk—for those times when someone does or says something kind of stupid. Just give 'em a good honk!

### Give your team some room to move
I've been at the restaurant now for over seven years, so I've had time to reconsider the limitations of my corner. I have also worked with many, many different people. In the beginning I was very territorial and would tell assistants where to stand and where everything went. Over the years I have found it more useful to encourage them to organize the space the way they feel is most efficient—as long as I can agree. This not only helps them develop their own sense of organization but also allows more free time for me to do what I consider to be my job—which is to produce, experiment, and ultimately keep moving forward at all times, no matter what it takes.

Ben Roche is Pastry Chef for Moto Restaurant in Chicago, Illinois. He is an interaction designer focusing on the intersection of technology and cuisine.

The chefs work in the Moto kitchen.

A well-stocked, readily available supply of building materials supports the attitudes "prototype toward a solution" and "bias toward action."

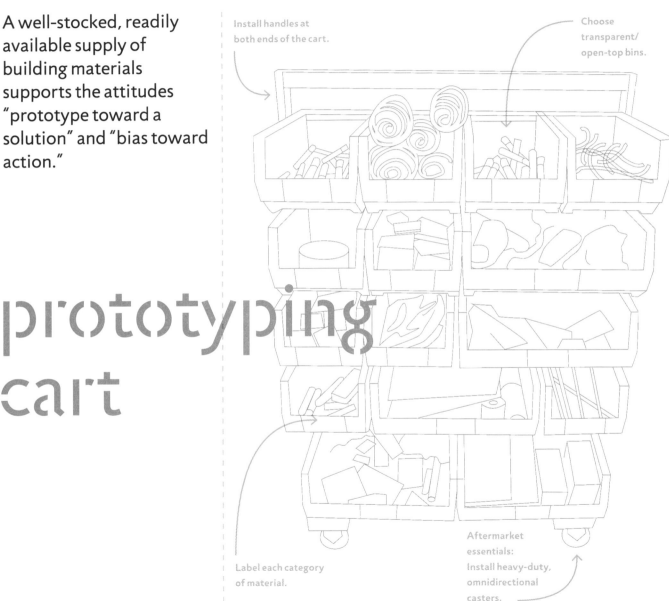

Install handles at both ends of the cart.

Choose transparent/open-top bins.

prototyping cart

Label each category of material.

Aftermarket essentials: Install heavy-duty, omnidirectional casters.

**The Prototyping Cart provides easy ways to inspire and explore ideas through building.**
At a glance it's a straightforward rolling supply center. It holds a lot of supplies and makes them accessible in a centralized & visible way uncommon to most work spaces. Making materials readily available is essential so that when people have ideas they instinctively embody them. Getting in touch with materials is a way to start exploring new ideas through low-resolution prototyping & testing.

**Keep the cart easy to access and readily maneuverable.**
Transparent containers for supplies are critical, so that people can always see what is available. Keep the Prototyping Cart in a prominent location and wheel it to where the action is. Having a meeting? Bring the Prototyping Cart with you.

**Stock your supplies in five categories:**
1. Pliable materials: rubber bands, modeling clay, tinfoil, and paper
2. Structural items: craft sticks, foam spheres, pipe cleaners, and wire
3. Connectors: painter's (blue) tape, white glue, staples, and binder clips
4. Utensils: scissors, staplers, hole punches, pens & pencils, including Sharpies
5. Treasure: decks of cards, toys, hats, stickers, and balloons

## build instructions

5' tall is an accessible height.

4' wide is not too cumbersome to move.

Choose bins that will fit through a doorway.

## tip

· Make sure to keep your cart well stocked & well organized. People immediately become frustrated when they discover that supplies are mislabeled or missing.

## sourcing

### carts
The d.school Prototyping Carts are sourced from Akro-Mils, Inc. (1293 South Main Street, Akron, OH 44301; 800 253-2467; www.akro-mils.com) and are identified as "Two-Sided Rail Racks."

### casters
Industrial Caster & Wheel Co. (2200 Carden Street, San Leandro, CA 94577; 510 569-8303; www.icwco.com). Reference Stanford d.school red caster in 3" or 5".
California Caster and Hand Truck Company (1400 17th Street, San Francisco, CA 94107; 800 950-8750; www.californiacaster.com)

## start

You can easily replicate the function of the Prototyping Carts using alternative containers: milk crates, plastic tubs, and bookshelves and bins. These containers can be centrally stored on shelves or in a bookcase on wheels: hack an IKEA shelving unit and add casters. To avoid the junk-drawer inertia, keep materials visible and organize them regularly.

## see also

**52**
Design Template_Attitudes: Bias toward Action

**53**
Design Template_Attitudes: Prototype toward a Solution

**108**
Tools_Full-Scale Space Prototyping Toolkit

**143**
Insights_Keep Supplies & Tools Visible for Inspiration & Instruction

**hack**

Place lines and materials on the floor to suggest separate activities or simulate full-scale experiences instantly.

Simple lines on the floor can create surprisingly powerful partitions that can be used to change behaviors & define boundaries. Use carpet tiles, paint, or tape to quickly suggest the footprint of a defined area. Tape on the floor is a cheap & easy way to audition new layouts. The cues from these visual boundaries separate one space from another, creating, for example, a lounge space within a work space or an enclosure within an open space.

## tips

· Use tape for quick experiments. Duct tape is useful, but it is often hard to remove from flooring. Try using blue painter's tape or masking tape. Other colors of tape can be employed to signal special boundaries.

· For more intentional projects, relatively inexpensive carpet tiles can be quickly attached to plywood, linoleum, and concrete floors using spray adhesive.

# instant boundaries from floor treatments

Special paint and stripes set apart parking for bikes. Palo Alto, CA

# open kitchen

**An open kitchen is an invitation to feel at home.**

**People spend a lot of time in the kitchen, so spend some money on it.** Party guests linger in the kitchen; the same is true at work. Make it a really pleasant place to be. Don't hesitate to spring for nice lighting, countertops, and cabinets.

**Provide space to sit and eat nearby.** The innovation design firm IDEO flanks its kitchen with big picnic tables. The strategic design firm SYPartners places the kitchen in a large shared space dotted with cafe-style tables.

**start**

A table or a watercooler can function as a kitchen-type anchor if your space won't accommodate appliances and such. Have benches nearby and keep simple snacks handy. Anchor your space with small, counter-top appliances like a toaster.

**Provide snacks and drinks.**
Strategically minded folks know that this keeps people around and working. The film industry provides constant access to food on shoots for just this reason. Better still, snacks keep people feeling fresh & engaged, and a visit to the kitchen provides a moment to chat. People will add to the pot. Once you set the tone, home-baked treats will start arriving (usually on Monday—post-weekend). Tea is a welcome beverage—it's warm, self-serve, and not too pricey. Nuts are a simple snack to stock—they are healthy and store well.

**The kitchen gets messy just like at home.**
You need a plan for cleanup. Whether you use a cleaning service or rely on community norms is up to you.

**Appliances.**
Outfitting a kitchen is pretty straight-forward, but don't skimp. Of course you'll need a coffeemaker and a fridge. An oven? It's handy to have a microwave but a toaster oven is even better—warm toasty treats are comforting. A watercooler that provides hot water is a must-have. Don't forget a sink, and maybe even a dishwasher, plus ample garbage cans so people can keep things tidy.

**see also**

41
Design Template_Places:
Gathering Spaces

41
Design Template_Places:
Thresholds/ Transitions

# Get There a Little Early, Leave a Little Late.

**Jay Cooney, assistant coach of the spectacular Stanford women's soccer team,\* always arrives at practice at least ten minutes early.**

Ten minutes prior to practice, the players are donning their cleats and warming up. This is an opportune time to chat casually, gauge how they are doing physically & emotionally, and work on little details that might not surface during the practice. This borrowed time is one of those little things that makes a big difference.

Even if you're the only one on the scene early, savor the moment alone: a little time to think between activities is a nice gift.

Leaving late has the same benefits, with a different flavor—a chance to chat and reflect on the event that just took place.

\* This is not a biased statement: As of the writing of the first edition, the Stanford Women's soccer team appeared in the NCAA finals 2 years running (2009 & 2010). They boasted 47 wins & only 2 losses in the same stretch.

## see also

### 120
Insights_Small Changes Can Have a Profound Impact

# Use Limits to Inspire Creativity.

**More flexible spaces require more limits.**

This is a bit counterintuitive. We initially experimented with spaces in which all the attributes were at play all the time. Everything from couches to walls was on casters—we had seemingly endless choices for desk size and height, for seating postures and arrangements. For a few people who were particularly attuned to space, this was creative nirvana. For many who just wanted to teach a class, this excessive supply of potential choices was paralyzing.

We've since limited the tweakable properties of our self-service spaces. With whiteboard panels rail-mounted on sliders, the only question is whether to use them or not. With a room full of identical square tables, users need only decide on a configuration.

**Limit the palate, of everything.**
There is something to be said for the beauty and grandiosity of a baroque, layered style, but it is not usually user-friendly. As the saying goes, you have to simplify to amplify.

Limiting types of furniture makes it easier to envision new configurations

for the space.

Limiting the amount & intensity of decoration allows signage to stand out.

Limiting the types of materials represented relaxes the brain by presenting a predictable pattern.

Limiting the number of different types of rooms within an environment creates a simple and accessible vocabulary of spaces that can be read and interpreted quickly for different purposes.

Limiting colors creates cohesion and an opportunity for a simple

vocabulary of signifiers. Use colors to denote different types of rooms, for instance.

## see also

# Storage Should Be at Least 30 Percent of Your Space.

**Whether you design for it or not, storage will take up at least 30 percent of your space.**

Creative spaces require storage: supplies, personal items, furniture that is not in use, inspirational objects, that thing we might need someday (you know the one). Treat storage as a living entity that occupies at least 30 percent of your space. You'll need at least that much.

**Storage is not stagnant.**
Storage should be as transparent as possible so that artifacts and concepts don't linger in the dark. Keep things visible to keep them in active use.

**Consider local off-site storage for seasonal-use items.**
This is a particularly handy approach as you shift between spaces in a land grab to grow out your current capacity.

Active storage &
work space in the
metal shop of
Lick-Wilmerding
High School.

make space

see also

174
Situations_Storage Gallery

220
Tools_Storage Towers

# The Cookie Rule

**Dessert is delicious. Dessert gets eaten. The Cookie Rule is this: People will eat as many cookies as are served.***

This rule is as true for any valuable asset as it is for a delicious treat. In our culture, storage space, whiteboards, and expendable items like foamboard, Post-its, prototyping supplies, coffee, and, of course, cookies fit the definition of delicious treats.

So what? It's important to be aware of what follows the Cookie Rule and provide accordingly. If you want those items to be used fluently, provide as many as possible and keep a buffer on hand for when you run out. If you want to change a behavior, find clever ways that allow you to limit usage.

*In some more polite cultures, the Cookie Rule has a slight caveat: People will eat as many cookies as are served, minus one. Some groups are bashful about eating the last cookie. We are not.

## see also

Dimensions: 36" wide x 36" deep x 60" high
Check your dimensions: adjust depth/width to
fit through critical doors!*

Helpful handles +
opportunity hooks

Non-precious
plywood surfaces

Lockable doors for
secure content

Big shelves
with adjustable
heights

# storage
# towers

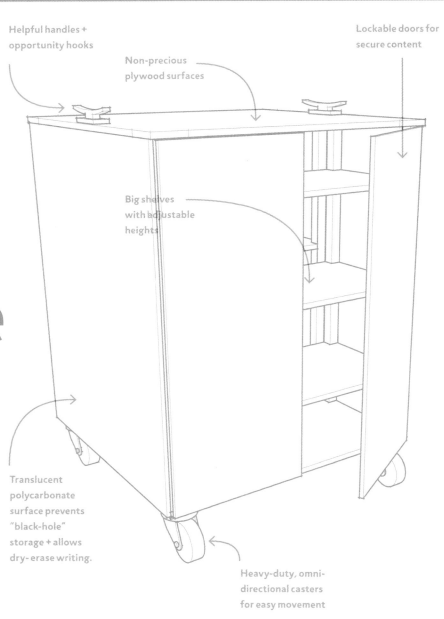

Translucent
polycarbonate
surface prevents
"black-hole"
storage + allows
dry- erase writing.

Heavy-duty, omni-
directional casters
for easy movement

# Redefine storage by placing your things front and center.

Moving storage for personal possessions and communal resources away from walls keeps those surfaces available for writing and creates new opportunities for using storage as a tool. Storage Towers are localized shelving units that create anchors within a space rather than at the margins—challenging the "out of sight, out of mind" behavior that often results in wasted space.

A build on the basic steamer trunk from the past, Storage Towers lend themselves to multiple configurations, including adjustable shelves, omni-directional casters, and removable or lockable doors. This flexibility allows you to take control of a space rather than just respond to inflexible features such as closets and cabinets.

\* The ADA standard in the United States for an interior door opening is 32" minimum. Double door openings without a center post will exceed this, while you may find openings in older buildings and residences that are less than 32".

Open-sided option for public display

## start

Try putting your small and large file cabinets on furniture-moving carts to enable you to reconsider permanent storage. Mount some industrial shelves on casters. Place the unit(s) in the middle of a room for a mobile partition and visible storage resource.

## sourcing

**manufacturing**

The Storage Towers were constructed by Stan Heick at HCSI Manufacturing (16890 Church Street, Building 7, Morgan Hill, CA 95037; 408 778-8231; www.hcsidesign.com).

**casters**

Industrial Caster & Wheel Co. (2200 Carden Street, San Leandro, CA 94577; 510 569-8303; www.icwco.com). Reference Stanford d.school red caster in 3" or 5".

California Caster and Hand Truck Company (1400 17th Street, San Francisco, CA 94107; 800 950-8750; www.californiacaster.com)

## see also

174
Situations_Storage Gallery

218
Insights_Storage Should Be at Least 30 Percent of Your Space

# Use Objects to Create Experiences.

**"Design is the art form that is incomplete until it is engaged."
—Matt Kahn**

**In other words, an object is only as useful as the experience it creates.** Designers can create beautiful objects, but the objects mean little unless they are useful. Take this idea further and measure the success of a design by the capabilities it creates.

**Identify the behaviors & capabilities you'd like to build within a space or a culture.** Curate the interactions among people and things to create those results. Take this approach with furniture, materials, and tools. When you choose a table, you also suggest the ways in which that table might be used and how it might lead to other activities. A worktable suggests building and creates a different engagement than a dining room table. Toys can encourage a playful culture, but even within that context, a foam basketball game creates a different engagement than a stack of Legos®. Begin thinking this way, and you'll start to see the potential actions in the shape, the fabric, and the height of the furniture you are selecting.

## see also

# Headphones Help Focus.

**In an open floor plan office, donning headphones says, "Please don't interrupt me."**

It's simple physics: the headphones raise the threshold of engagement and provide a license to ignore. Anyone who has worked in an open floor plan office is well aware of this—it's the equivalent of shutting the office door.

    This signal works pretty well but can make for an outwardly quiet space. This may or may not be what you want. If it works for your culture, consider giving folks headphones as part of the entry ritual to the space—it's a nice touch and helps set the norm.

## see also

**132**
Situations_Hiding Place

**196**
Insights_The Open Office Floor Plan Has a Shadow

# the coffee shop

A tall, long, and narrow table is an excellent platform for creating a coffee shop vibe.

**To support individual work but preserve collaborative intersections, create a place to work alone, together.**
The coffee shop as a place to meet & work has long been a haven for individual creative workers. As we write this book, coffee shop–like co-working spaces with open-plan seating and desk space, self-serve kitchens, and drop-in meeting spaces are flourishing.

**When this model works well, you get the best of both worlds.**
People actually get work done in this type of space, but they also benefit from collaborative collisions: quick tips, feedback, visibility into others' work & working styles.

**Downsides.**
In places where many folks are working on projects together or the social norm is interruption, such open work space can be distracting. Conversations can interrupt focused, "heads down" work, driving people to work elsewhere. Too

quiet, and you lose the potential energy of others. Both ends of the spectrum squelch the original motivation for having shared space. Regular reflection on how things are going helps set or reset social behaviors.

**There are some subtleties in creating a good coffee shop vibe within a working organization.**

**Home base**
People who depend on the coffee shop also need a mini home base to store tools & reference materials, personal keepsakes, and work in progress. Think: a dependable place to sit and a counter or desk with wall space & storage.

**Choices**
It is unproductive & unhealthy to sit in one position for too long. Laptops and their ilk make it easy for work to move. Seating variations allow people to easily shift working styles and postures. Dot the space with comfortable lounge chairs, tall workbenches, communal tables, and isolated desks.

**Private space**
In an open-office plan, the need for privacy does not disappear; there are calls to make and secrets to share. Surround the open-plan work space with several options for private, tuck-in space.

## start

Try it out: Take over a space that can function as an open-plan work area: a lobby, a hallway, or a large workroom. Get a few others to work there for a week or so and see how it goes. What would you need to make it work—physically and socially?

## see also

40
Design Template_Places:
Home Base

41
Design Template_Places:
Gathering Spaces

196
Insights_The Open Office Floor Plan
Has a Shadow

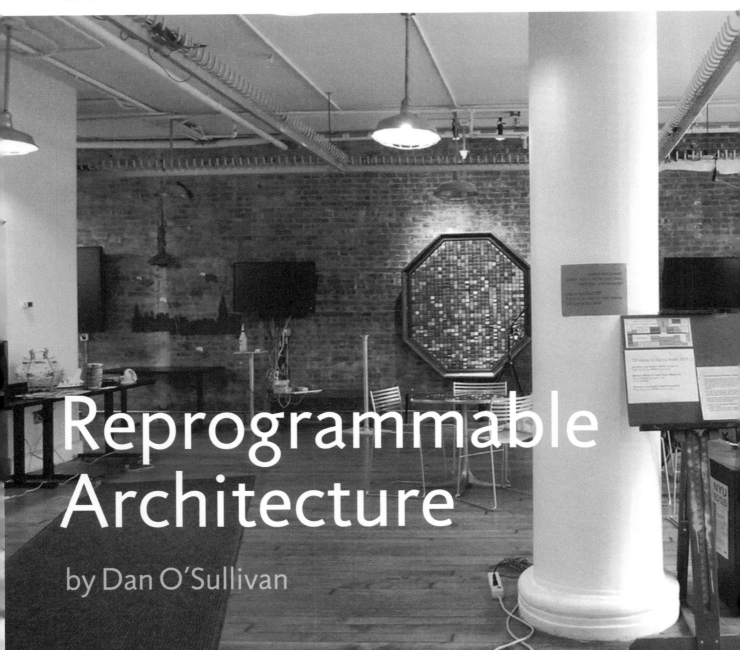

# Reprogrammable Architecture

by Dan O'Sullivan

# Space Studies_Reprogrammable Architecture

## Architectural Wannabes

Interactive media had a lot to learn from architecture. Red Burns started the Interactive Telecommunications Program (ITP) in a film school focused on storytelling. As the random-access memory of personal computers came into the picture, spatial disciplines like architecture became better models than linear disciplines like screenwriting. With computers, the interest was more in creating a space, as architects do, where multiple stories can transpire. Five years after ITP began, the MIT Media Lab came out of the School of Architecture. This connection between interactive media and architecture might explain why faculty and students at ITP can't seem to stop fiddling with our physical space.

## Software Culture

ITP tends to be more experimental than vocational, but after fifteen years of existence, our graduates finally fit into the job title of "Information Architect." No sooner did that happen than software culture came into its own and the architectural metaphor began to feel too heavy. In software culture, failure is more of an option, precedent can be more of an enemy than a friend, and user testing is more efficient than critique. Now architecture might have some things to learn from this software culture. What if our physical spaces were as easily reallocated as computer memory?

left: Bare boards before the start of the semester at ITP.

above: Student projects and activity erupting throughout the space.

## User Generated

Twice a year our floor starts out completely bare—nothing on the walls, the tables in an orderly grid. Gradually the space grows a lining of people inhabiting various corners with their laptops. We have a grid on the ceiling for relocating lights, the furniture has wheels, and the screens are all installed on swivels. There is a big pile of pipes, curtains, boards, and clamps inviting student use. This giant "erector set" sits exposed in a corner of a room because closet walls were among the first things to go. The idea of "display your storage" has not only reclaimed space from storage of useless junk, it has provoked projects when students see useful but previously hidden stuff.

As student projects progress and require more structure, tables and lights are moved or built, and poles and curtains start to go up, until the floor looks like a shantytown. At the end of the semester we clean things up a bit and clear out some lanes for thousands of people to walk through during our two-day show. Minutes after the last visitor has left, the students work together like an organized colony of ants, and, inconceivably, in two hours the floor is stripped and reset to its original bare state. These cycles give the students ownership and invite their creativity into every nook of the floor. The summer is then the season to move some of the more permanent walls to conform to the new flows.

## Our Beams and Deans

Of course, architecture is not yet as malleable as software. The tougher structure to work around for people trying to build a space like ours is usually bureaucracy. And massive institutions like New York University cannot suddenly trust a bottom-up approach. Construction money and energy are typically budgeted to be spent in a short period of time at the launch of a program, but experimentation and learning should happen every year. Over the past three decades we have developed a trust with our dean's office whereby they expect us to change 10 percent of our space every summer and never ask for a complete overhaul. We are blessed with the simple loft structure of columns every sixteen feet and material in between that is relatively inexpensive and, we hope, ecologically changeable.

Dan O'Sullivan is Chair of ITP (Interactive Telecommunications Program) at New York University's Tisch School of the Arts.

The space
reprogrammed
to suit
student work.

Borrowed from the theater, an overhead grid is invaluable in a space designed to adapt to changing scenes.

# grid system

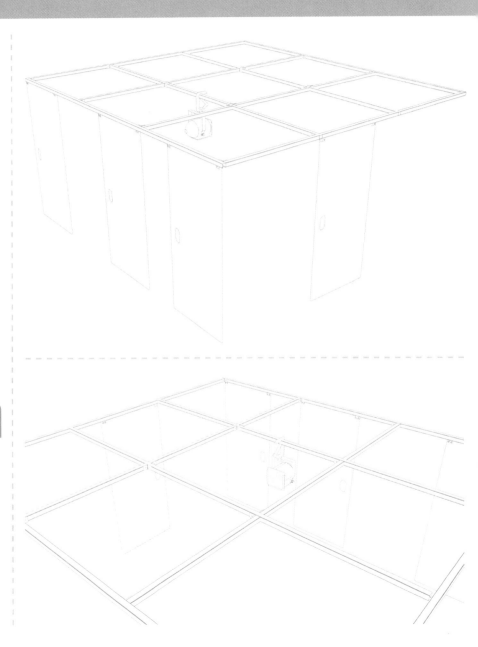

A grid supports rapid setup of team spaces and infrastructure for storage & display of project work. The exact construction of a grid system can vary greatly, though it is critical to keep it easy to access & engage. Key aspects are quick & easy connections and a scale large enough to support the physical work from several teams.

A heavy-duty grid is perfect for supporting deployable dry-erase surfaces; these can range from simple panels built from showerboard and plywood to polycarbonate sheets. A light-duty grid of cable/rope/PVC pipe is excellent for quickly mounting sheet material such as foamboard and large-format craft paper.

Connection should be as easy as hanging clothespins on a backyard laundry line. Your connector options vary widely depending on the grid you install. Many manufacturers, such as Unistrut, make metal connectors with multiple functions. Tape, hangers, and binder clips are quite effective as well. For more connection inspiration, explore the variety of hook options at any hardware store or home center.

## sourcing

**steel**
Unistrut (www.unistrut.com) offers steel materials with many standard connection options. Unistrut in the San Francisco Bay Area: Lord & Sons (430 East Trimble Road, San Jose, CA 95131; 800 468-3791; www.lordandsons.com).

**aluminum**
80/20 Inc. (1701 South 400 East, Columbia City, IN 46725; www.8020.net) supplies aluminum materials with many precision function options.

**etc**.
PVC pipe, laundry lines, and wire-cable/rope/yarn materials are available at most hardware stores and home centers.

## start

Install eye hooks (at stud locations) on opposite walls in a room, and string a wire cable across the space. Include a turnbuckle for tightening the cable. Use binder clips to attach foamboard or other sheet material for display. Next step: Install a length of Unistrut channel in two directions across a small room. (You'll likely need some engineering help with this one.) Construct simple dry-erase surfaces and install using standard hardware.

## see also

**20**
Situations_Instant/Shared Studio

**48**
Design Template_Actions: Saturate

**58**
Tools_Whiteboard Sliders

Spring-loaded studs provide instant vertical support that can be used in place of a wall for most nonstructural uses—from defining team spaces to displaying work.

# jacks

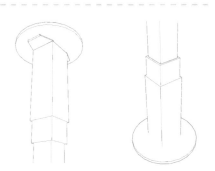

Jacks take their name from their cousins in heavy construction. In that context, jacks are used to carry heavy loads from above. The jacks we use are lightweight poles that extend from the floor to overhead support—a beam or a solid ceiling.

The installation of jacks quickly facilitates opportunities to display foamboard panels or Short Boards. You can also use them to create vertical storage opportunities, saving valuable wall space for dry-erase surfaces. Pop up a set of three or four jacks next to each other and mount a few hooks for storing foam panels. Quickly subdivide your space by attaching any sheet materials between jacks; these impromptu partitions can be short- or long-term installations.

The range of modifications is limited only by the material selected for the vertical piece and includes attachments such as eye hooks and drilled holes, which offer a wealth of possibilities for creating and partitioning microspaces within a much larger environment. Vertical components constructed of basic materials such as wood or metal/ PVC pipe allow you to tailor your space for short- or long-term needs.

## sourcing

**wood**
Standard 2x2 lumber is available at any lumberyard or home center. Select straight pieces with few, if any, knots.

**hardware**
Furniture levelers and other hook and hardware attachments are available at hardware stores. McMaster-Carr (600 N. County Line Road, Elmhurst, IL 60126; 630 600-3600; www.mcmaster.com) has an excellent selection of different materials in a range of sizes.

**attachments**
The d.school currently uses custom top and bottom attachments designed in collaboration with Steelcase. The top attachment is spring-loaded to lock into standard Unistrut channels or press against flat ceilings.

## start

Source some 2x2 lumber and trim it to approximately ceiling-to-floor length. Attach heavy-duty furniture levelers at the jack bases. Adjust for a very tight friction fit. Start with standard hardware hooks to hold foamboard panels. Experiment with different types of hardware to explore use-case possibilities.

## see also

**174**
Situations_Storage Gallery

**200**
Tools_Short Boards

**240**
Tools_Connectors

Attach furniture levelers to the top and bottom of a length of 2x2.

# modular multiples

**Multiples of modular tools make an easier scene to craft and navigate.**

We've tried outfitting a room with four or five different types of tables and seats designed to accommodate any situation in a room . . . at the same time. It seemed like a good thing to do: provide options. Wrong. More frequently, when users are pressed for time (which is always), the abundance of options complicates things. The lesson: Use multiples of the same type of tools in a given room. Limit choice to one or two types of seats and one or two types of tables to create a comprehensible landscape to set up and to engage.

**start**

Limit yourself to one type of table per room. Gang smaller tables together to create different surface configurations.

**see also**

**28**
Tools_Periodic Table

**217**
Insights_Use Limits to Inspire Creativity

make space

# Platform vs. Application

**In software, there is a distinction between a platform and an application. Applications support specific tasks; platforms are environments built to run applications. Think of space as a platform for creative collaboration.**

Buildings have always been platforms for enabling all kinds of applications. This hasn't changed. The shift is in the nature of the applications. But the job of a space designer is shifting. Buzzwords notwithstanding—do-it-yourself, maker, participatory media, creator culture, this or that 2.0—right now it is about empowering people to make and take action. Space design is particularly attuned to this goal.

**Instead of designing for users, think also of designing for designers.**
Users is an awkward term at best—it evokes images of junkies, needles, and decrepit alleyways. In designing for designers, focus on empowering rather than solving. In a computer program-ming context the closest analogy is creating an API* for your physical space. How does the platform you create allow people to make modifica-tions either in response to an existing application or in search of something new? How can you make spaces hackable?

*API = application programming interface: roughly, a set of protocols and commands that allow programmers to interface with a piece of software to develop new extensions and applica-tions using its functionality.

## see also

**22**
Insights_Context Is Content

**40**
Design Template_Places

Conceptual tools, like Imagination Playground pieces, move from abstract toward specific resolution.

# Steal from the Black Box Theater.

**Simple spaces with suggestive objects and materials bring people into focus and provide room to work out ideas as they emerge.**

**A black box theater is a small theater, simply housed in any large room.**
It is an excellent guiding metaphor for any creative space.

**The finish of the space communicates only the absence of itself.**
Walls and floors are painted black. The floor is often skinned with wood for easy attachment. A stage sits at floor level with close seats on three or four sides. Rigging for lights & sets hangs from the ceiling. When used for rehearsal, there is a minimal palette of props: primarily black cubes to sit, lie, or stand on. Tape on the floor suggests locations for future boundaries and props.

**The focus of a black box is on simple functionality rather than prescriptive use.**
There is nothing much to it, but the potential is incredibly special—as soon as you set foot inside, you know something is going to happen. The unadorned space brings people into focus. The ambiguity of props leaves room for the imagination as they adapt to contexts set by users—for example, wood blocks can become a wall as easily as a countertop. An arrangement of chairs can represent a building lobby or a new customer experience. This approach is especially helpful in spaces that are used for working out ideas on a human scale (e.g., service-oriented solutions).

**Should you paint a room black? Probably not.**
Use the metaphor to consider your own space in terms of minimum needs, props, and support. What is the minimum palette of objects your creative spaces need to be effective?

**Space needs:** How much room do you really need in which to create? How might you use an empty office or hallway to workshop ideas?

**Props & support:** What type of rigging, props or support structure do you need? What sorts of lighting, audio, and partitioning tools can you hack together?

## see also

18
Tools_Foam Cubes

108
Tools_Full-Scale Space Prototyping Toolkit

118
Tools_Scoop Stool

180
Tools_Bleacher Blocks

The Black Box Theatre at the Rustaveli National Theatre, Tbilisi, Georgia.

# Design for the Beginning, Middle, & End

**We experience life in sequence. So think about the sequences at play when designing a space.**

By definition, space has three dimensions, but the fourth dimension—time—is critical in understanding any experience within a space.

We've got the ancient Greeks to thank for their insight that provides a convenient framework: the arc of a story. Since the days of Aristotle, dramatic arcs have been described as having a beginning, a middle, and an end.

What is the story arc of the engagement of a space? How do you design for all three of these phases? The beginning: the entry, the welcome, the arrival, the engagement. The middle: the activity, the action. The end: the wrap, the goodbye, the cleanup, the exit.

## see also

176
Insights_Recognize Your Emotional Arc during a Project

216
Insights_Get There a Little Early, Leave a Little Late

Seeing the movie is only one part of the experience at the Los Angeles Theatre.

Keep a variety of
connectors handy to
encourage modification
of spaces.

Prototype
connectors,
designed by the
d.school & Dave
Shipman,
Steelcase Custom
Products Group.

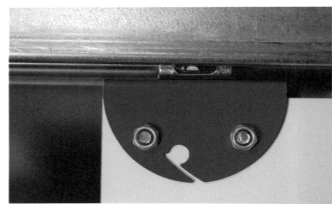

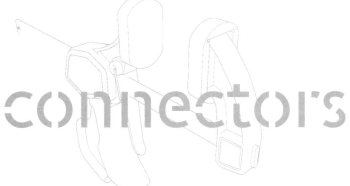

connectors

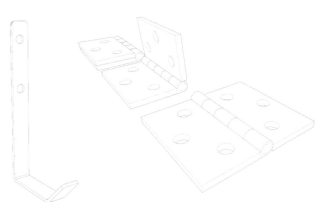

Connectors are a good thing to have around. Paired with sheet material and other simple components, they can become a platform for altering existing spaces or for fabricating new ones. Connectors send a strong signal that the space can (and should) be modified.

Connectors are cues for strength in your space: sturdy metal hooks, heavy-duty clamps, and strong hinges not only convey confidence, they actually stand up to countless use cycles as well as abuse, whether intentional or accidental. Providing these types of resources fosters a culture of building by encouraging people not only to physically embody their ideas, but also to respond to and engage with their physical surroundings.

The d.school has designed and manufactured a number of simple custom parts in collaboration with Steelcase and other local manufacturers. These parts—including pegs, hinges, clamps, and tubes—are fine-tuned versions of standard components you can find in the aisles of hardware stores.

**starter kit**

· Clamps: Quick-clamps are incredibly versatile tools for connecting parts and mounting components. Pony A-shaped spring clamps are cheap and easy tools to use for mounting sheet materials to just about anything.

· Tape: Tape is the quintessential quick connector. It also works brilliantly as a hinge to connect sheet materials. Duct tape is nice, but it leaves residue. Opt for blue painter's tape. It is strong, it can be easily repositioned, and it looks cool.

· Stanley L-shaped hooks can hold 50 lb when mounted to a wood stud. They extend 4" or 5" from the mounting surface and can be used to hold Short Boards, mount shelves, store tools, and hang coats.

· The Unistrut Trolley (Part P2949) is a sliding part that works in conjunction with Unistrut channels that can be wall- or ceiling-mounted. Essentially tiny roller skates, these parts can attach to any sheet materials large or small (plywood, showerboard, foamboard) to create movable and deployable work surfaces.

· Stanley heavy-duty brass hinges make connecting sheet materials, such as plywood, very easy. Hinges can allow you to build sturdy structures quickly without having to worry about refined wood joinery. Hinges also allow you to add dynamic features to your spaces—expandable wall panels, for example.

· Stock up on fasteners such as screws, bolts, nuts, and washers to make installing your connectors quick and easy. Try to keep a consistent inventory of sizes (lengths, diameters, and thread sizes), so you can easily assemble, disassemble, and reuse parts. Self-tapping screws (such as sheet metal screws) are fantastic, as they allow you to insert screws without first drilling a pilot hole.

**start**

Walk the aisles of a store near you and select several different types of connectors. Buy a few of each type for consistency & keep them available. Install hooks along an unused wall and mount a piece of foamboard. Watch what activities arise & see how you can support them with more options.

**sourcing**

**connectors**
Your local hardware store or the hardware aisles of retail home centers are excellent resources for connectors of all sorts. McMaster-Carr (600 North County Line Road, Elmhurst, IL 60126; 630 600-3600; www.mcmaster.com) is an online source for an incredible array of connectors, including the clamps, hooks, and hinges mentioned here.

**steel**
Unistrut (www.unistrut.com) offers steel materials with many standard connection options. Unistrut in the San Francisco Bay Area: Lord & Sons (430 East Trimble Road, San Jose, CA 95131; 800 468-3791; www.lordandsons.com).

**aluminum**
80/20 Inc. (1701 South 400 East, Columbia City, IN 46725; www.8020.net) supplies aluminum materials with many precision function options.

Tables define how and where you work. That is, when you want to work at a table. When you don't, tables take up a frustrating amount of space. Build tables that are easy to move and break down.

Sometimes the available choices don't fit either your physical space or the values of your culture. What type of table accurately represents your culture? Ping-Pong? Circular? Square? Fold-up? If a Ping-Pong table works for you, then your sporting goods store is also your furniture store.

Explore these quick & inexpensive ways to set up your space. Use them as the basis of your furniture system, or experiment with them before moving on to something more elaborate.

# quick component tables

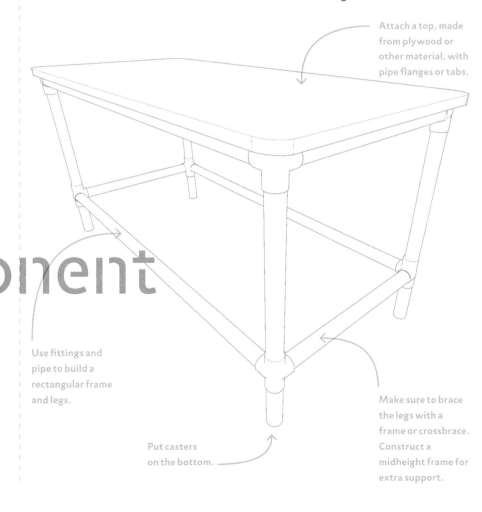

Attach a top, made from plywood or other material, with pipe flanges or tabs.

Use fittings and pipe to build a rectangular frame and legs.

Put casters on the bottom.

Make sure to brace the legs with a frame or crossbrace. Construct a midheight frame for extra support.

## build instructions

### option 1:
### Aluminum Pipe Construction (pictured)

Pipes & pipe fittings make a handy construction kit for any piece of furniture. Specialty aluminum pipe is especially suitable because it is light, easy to cut, and available in many finishes. Table bases made of pipe take a bit more setup and can't be broken down quickly, although they can be completely disassembled and their parts reused as needed. Large-diameter (2"+) PVC pipe is a cheaper and easier-to-trim alternative but is less sturdy and less attractive.

- Use slip-on pipe fittings for quick release.
- Desk height = approximately 29".
- Counter height = approximately 36".
- Bar (standing) height = approximately 40".

Pipe + pipe fitting

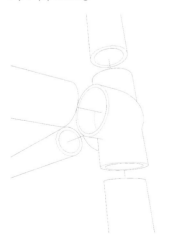

### option 2:
### Component Legs & Tops

Buy tables in component parts. For instance, IKEA sells most tabletops separately from legs. You can mix and match their components or components from another source. Although these are less convenient for quick setup and breakdown, they are great for all kinds of hacking and experimentation. For instance, add a plywood box between the top and the legs and you can re-create a table not unlike the Periodic Table.

## sourcing

Your local home center will have sawhorses, sheet material, and hollow-core doors.

### pipe
Speedrail is a manufacturer of specialty aluminum pipe; this material is available through Hollaender Mfg. (P.O. Box 156399, 10285 Wayne Avenue, Cincinnati, OH 45215; 800 772-8800; www.hollaender.com).

### tabletops/legs
IKEA (www.ikea.com) has a large selection of tabletops and legs.

## see also

### 28
Tools_Periodic Table

## start

Architecture students have been doing this right for decades: straddle a piece of plywood or a door across two sawhorses. Simple. Home supply stores sell inexpensive, hollow-core doors that are lightweight & sturdy. The "door aesthetic" is not for everybody, however; they often come with a precut hole for the door handle. Nevertheless, they are big and reasonably priced, and thus can be a good utilitarian option.

Any sawhorse will do, but one with adjustable legs is nice to have in case you want to change heights. Powder-coated metal legs and a piece of sealed or stained plywood look surprisingly nice if you're willing to spend a bit more.

# Provide Permission: Say "Yes," Mostly

**One way to think of space design is as an embodiment of a particular set of permissions.**

From this point of view, your design goal is to create spaces that make it easy to engage in behaviors your community believes are important. Keep this perspective front of mind as you are faced with the countless decisions that go into designing a space.

Take it further still: empower people to alter their space. This will enlist them in the creation of the space, bring new ideas to fruition, and keep the space evolving.

However, beware of the potential downsides of too much modification: conflict & a loss of coherency. In designing possibilities, you also need to consider limits. Embrace this notion— it's just as important to your culture as making things easy. In many cases, limits will make things easier by reducing the complexity inherent in unbridled choice.

Warning: performing music is strictly permitted at Vondelpark in Amsterdam. Yes!

## see also

**203**
Insights_Patina Gives Permission

**217**
Insights_Use Limits to Inspire Creativity

Is molten bronze okay for the foundry floor of Stanford's Product Realization Lab? Of course.

# Flooring Shapes Creative Activities.

**Choose underfoot material carefully when considering the attitudes and activities that you want to support in your space.**

The character of concrete suggests that it is non-precious & strong, and an exposed concrete floor supports a disposition toward building and making mistakes— trying things! In contrast, hardwood floors subtly cue less messy behavior by creating warmth and intimacy through visual appearance, underfoot feel, and acoustic dampening.

Carpeting is the standard default for all manner of work spaces. It's soft, has appealing acoustic properties, and comes in a huge variety of looks. In creative spaces, consider using it highly intentionally, if not very sparingly. Dropping a permanent marker on concrete is an "oops," while doing the same to carpet is an "I didn't do it."

## see also

37
Insights_Expose Raw Materials

121
Insights_Use Soft Boundaries to Partition Open Spaces

# defaults

Have a clear default configuration for shared spaces. Show people who use the space how to leave it for others.

### In a prescriptive "single-use" drop-in space:
You should be able to engage the default immediately. What needs to be in place so that the space can be used with minimal setup? How should it be arranged? How restocked?

### In a flexible/self-service space:
The default should be somewhat of a "clean-slate," an easy-to-engage but nearly empty space. Include some suggestive elements that can be put to use quickly, but keep them easy to rearrange.

### Label defaults clearly.
Use BIG signs to label the default configuration of the space. Employ layouts and photos combined with a clear, simple bulleted list to walk people through the protocol of resetting the space.

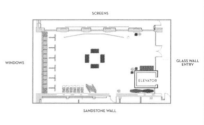

Graphical and text instructions posted prominently help people reset spaces & set norms for use.

## start

Define a default for one of your shared spaces using either the single-use drop-in or the flexible self-service models as described. Communicate the new default through every channel you have—create visual signs, inform people face-to-face, and notify them via e-mail.

### see also

92
Tools_Signs That POP

94
Tools_Vinyl Cutter

# The Escalator Test

"An escalator can't break, it can only become stairs."
—Mitch Hedberg, comedian

**The Escalator Test is a useful gut-check.**

When sorting through options, ask the simple question: "What will this do when it is not in use?"

Take two options for digital whiteboard capture: an analog whiteboard with a camera capture and a digital, screen-based drawing board that captures on the go. There are plenty of reasons to go with one or the other. The Escalator Test says go with the analog whiteboard plus camera option; it can't break; it can only become a regular whiteboard.

Although it's not applicable to every item—a laptop is an indispensable tool even though it's nothing more than an ill-proportioned paperweight when it's turned off—the Escalator Test is a useful evaluation tool in many situations.

## see also

**203**
Insights_Patina Gives Permission

# It's about People

**Shed your assumptions about what work is and notice what people are really doing in your space.**

**Creative "work" rarely describes a single activity.**
In fact, "thinking" often happens in unlikely places (for instance, while commuting to work or taking a shower). Observations of people at work at the d.school reveals shifts in modes from typing to sketching, building, taking pictures, talking with others, grabbing coffee, and even taking a nap.

**Get inspiration from work-arounds & hacks.**
Creative work spaces are rife with little modifications to make work easier or more enjoyable. We've seen everything from using windowpanes to sort sticky notes to improvised desktop kitchenettes complete with toaster ovens stashed underneath. These examples are clues about unmet needs and potential solutions. Build on and around what you notice.

**Look to bridge the discrepancies between what people say and what they do.**
Gaps between what people say and what they do are rich sources of inspiration. One person might insist that he doesn't need much room to work. Yet you notice that in actuality he occupies several work spaces and leaves piles of unfinished tasks in his wake. This suggests that he has an unmet need, whether or not he realizes it. It also suggests that he feels a sense of ownership over a shared space. These simple observations provide a wealth of opportunity for design intervention.

## see also

# The Environments Collaborative

Charlotte

Lia

Joel

George

Scott

Rich

Michal

The Environments Collaborative is a group at the Stanford University d.school responsible for developing and experimenting with collaborative spaces in service of student, staff, and visitor experiences. This group, like many at the d.school, draws from full-time staff and an extended network of friendly designers & builders to tackle the ambiguous challenge of using space to support innovation. Like our student teams, the Environments Collaborative leverages the multi disciplinary skills of these incredibly talented individuals. The Environments Collaborative ultimately is the ever-so-motley crew challenged with designing, building, and often cleaning the d.school environment.

**Malte Jung** is a design researcher in the field of mechanical engineering. His work focuses on the emotional dynamics of teams embedded in design work.
Birch Hall, Sweet Hall

**Scott Doorley** is currently Co-Director of the Environments Collaborative at the Stanford d.school. He is a serious dabbler, who rarely dabbles in seriousness. His educational and professional backgrounds include filmmaking, design, and education.
Birch Hall, Sweet Hall, Bldg. 524, Bldg. 550

**Dave Baggeroer** is an engineer, a designer, and an entrepreneur with a passion for making in physical and digital media. He is currently designing social software for mobile phones.
Sweet Hall, Bldg. 524, Bldg. 550

**Natalie Woyzbun** is an artist and designer with an educational background in Curatorial Studies. She is keenly interested in the details of interaction design and is currently developing inspiration tools for creative and design professionals.
Sweet Hall, Bldg. 524, Bldg. 550

**Carly Geehr** has a background in mechanical engineering and product design. She is passionate about solving problems through direct action and building. Carly is currently developing entrepreneurial platforms in the fields of volunteerism and food design.
Bldg. 524

**Adam Royalty** is Lead Research Investigator at the Stanford d.school. When he's not playing the role of trickster, he applies his experience in the fields of math and education, with a focus on design, to understand the impact of design thinking.
Birch Hall, Sweet Hall, Bldg. 524, Bldg. 550

**Alex Ko** is a graphic and product designer with extensive applied experience in interior and architectural design. His early-age interests in toys and tools for embodying design are evident in his current entrepreneurial work in design and branding.
Birch Hall, Sweet Hall, Bldg. 524

**Bruce Boyd** is Director of Technology at the Stanford d.school. With each new day he adds to his 15 years of entrepreneurial experience in innovating on engagements that bring people and technology together.
Birch Hall, Sweet Hall, Bldg. 524, Bldg. 550

**Joel Sadler** is a mechanical engineer and a designer focused on social entrepreneurship in the field of prosthetic augmentations. He is a child of Jamaica, with dreams of rocket ships and electric sheep.
Bldg. 524, Bldg. 550

**Charlotte Burgess-Auburn** is Director of Community at the Stanford d.school. She uses her background in art, art history, and theater production to design the d.school engagement experience for all student and staff teams.
Birch Hall, Sweet Hall, Bldg. 524, Bldg. 550

**Lia Siebert** has an educational background in business and mechanical engineering. She has actively applied both of these contexts to designing for people. Her work encompasses the fields of medical device design, design education, and entrepreneurial design development in Latin America.
Sweet Hall, Bldg. 524, Bldg. 550

**George Kembel** is Executive Director and Co-Founder of the Stanford d.school. He is an engineer, designer, and entrepreneur focused on amplifying and accelerating the impact of design on the lives of students at Stanford and around the world.
Durand, Birch Hall, Sweet Hall, Bldg. 524, Bldg. 550

**Scott Witthoft** is currently Co-Director of the Environments Collaborative at the Stanford d.school. He is sometimes an artist, always a maker. His educational and professional backgrounds include civil and structural engineering and product design.
Bldg. 524, Bldg. 550

**Michal Kopec** is an engineer and designer focused on entrepreneurial methods for global good. His work focuses on digital and physical interaction design.
Birch Hall, Sweet Hall, Bldg. 524

**Rich Crandall** is Director of the K–12 Laboratory at the Stanford d.school. He is a puzzler: a current treasure hunter and a former high school math teacher. Rich applies his business mindedness and design sensibilities to the challenge of reinventing K–12 education.
Birch Hall, Sweet Hall, Bldg. 524, Bldg. 550

Through their own independent convictions and commitments, these special individuals have invaluably aided the work of the Environments Collaborative. Their unique and powerful contributions embodied in the acts of physically building and iterating spaces in the service of teaching and learning have helped shape the d.school experience for all:

**Bernie Roth**
**James M. Patell**
**James G. Patell**
**Erica Estrada**
**Kerry O'Connor**
**Alex Kazaks**
**Rick Ellinger**
**Charlie Ellinger**
**David Klaus**

For teaching me, among other things, to build

# from Scott Witthoft:

My parents, Thomas and Sandra
My brothers, Jeffrey and Theodore

My friends and my family

For the countless opportunities

For believing in me & giving me room to grow

# from Scott Doorley:

My parents, Gail & Tom
My brother, Chris

My wife, Rachelle

My daughters

For your precision & wit

For endless surprises

For being my friends and my family

For helping me believe in myself

# Acknowledgments

*For this book*

from
Scott Doorley
and Scott
Witthoft:

Grace Hawthorne

George Kembel
David Kelley
Bernie Roth
Sarah Stein Greenberg

*For all of
your work in
supporting
the d.school
and our goals*

Hasso Plattner
Brit d'Arbeloff
Mike Levinthal

Lia Siebert
Erica Estrada
Corey Ford
Joel Sadler
Thomas Both
Jeremy Utley
Rich Crandall
Caroline O'Connor
Alex Ko
Kerry O'Connor
David Baggeroer
Adam Royalty

Julian Gorodsky
Bruce Boyd
Charlotte Burgess-Auburn
Susie Wise

Charlie Ellinger
Tammy Goodall
Kim Kendall-Humphreys
Natalie Glatzel
Erika Basu
Uri Geva
Debbe Stern

Bob Sutton
Terry Winograd
Jim Patell
Tina Seelig
Debra Dunn
Perry Klebahn
Chris Flink
Bill Moggridge
Alex Kazaks

Liz Gerber
Scott Klemmer
James Monsees
Brian Witlin
Colter Leyes
Adam French
Enrique Allen
Jay Cooney
Nicole Kahn
Meg Lee
Weiying Yu
Susan Hosking Ramos
Anne Fletcher
Jennifer Tackman
Geoff Kembel

Kim Saxe
Andrew Salverda
Yusuke Miyashita
Dave Beach

*For your
ceaseless
enthusiasm*

Craig Milroy
Elysa Fenenbock
Andrew Taylor
Daniel Steinbock
Jonathan Edelman

Ed Howard
Mike Drez
Frank Graziano
David Shipman
Julie Barnhart Hoffman
Jim Hackett

Jim Plummer
Sandy Meyer
Helena Cipres-Palacin
Brian Carilli
David Kirk
Bob Wheeler
Laura Breyfogle
Elaine Glatzel
Chris Crismon
Chris Wasney
Kaori Abiko
Matt Pietras
Rachelle Fernandez

Scott Stowell
Todd Hido
Mark Rutherford
William Mercer McLeod
Margaret Cummins
Derek Fagerstrom

The students of the d.school

This Page Unintentionally Left Blank

make space

# Colophon

### design

**make space** was designed by Open (www.notclosed.com). Scott Stowell, Yoshie Hozumi, Adam Katz, Catherine Kirk, Naz Sahin, Jules Tardy, Ryan Thacker, and Amit Werber all contributed to the project.

The programs used included Adobe InDesign CS5, Illustrator CS5, and Photoshop CS5.

The authors and designers used additional resources in generating & sourcing visual elements, including Apple TextEdit, Google SketchUp, flickr, WikiMedia Commons, and digital photography.

### typography

**make space** is typeset in Jigsaw, a type family designed in 1999 by Johanna Balusikova and published by Typotheque, a type foundry based in The Hague, the Netherlands.

### photography

The cover photographs are by Todd Hido (www.toddhido.com)

Additional photographs, where noted: William Mercer McLeod

# Colophon

## production

Grace Hawthorne

Making anything, including a book, requires vision and attention to detail. Grace Hawthorne brought both to bear to inspire this book and to bring it to fruition.

## printing

The first edition of **make space** was printed by RR Donnelly in Crawfordsville, IN.

## paper

The cover for **make space** is 15pt. Carolina C1S Cover by International Paper.

Paper is 70# Lynx.

# yellow pages

**aluminum rail & components**
80/20 Inc. (www.8020.net)

**cameras, lighting & audio**
Abel Cine (877 880-4267;
   www.abelcine.com)
Adolf Gasser Photography (415 495-4365;
   www.gassersphoto.com)
B&H Photo & Video (800 606-6969;
   www.bhphotovideo.com)
JCX Expendables (415 824-4110;
   www.jcxex.com)
Samy's Camera (310 450-4365;
   www.samys.com)
Talamas Broadcast Equipment (617 928-0788;
   www.talamas.com)

**cardboard boxes**
U-Haul (www.uhaul.com)

**carpet**
FLOR (866 952-4093; www.flor.com)

**carts (prototyping bins)**
Akro-Mils, Inc. (800 253-2467;
   www.akro-mils.com)

**carts & panel trucks**
Grainger (800 323-0620;
   www.grainger.com)

**casters**
Industrial Caster & Wheel Co. (510 569-8303;
   www.icwco.com)
California Caster and Hand Truck Company
   (800 950-8750;
   www.californiacaster.com)
McMaster-Carr (630 600-3600;
   www.mcmaster.com)

**coffee**
Sightglass (415 861–1313;
   www.sightglasscoffee.com)
Four Barrel (415 252-0800;
   www.fourbarrelcoffee.com)
Ritual Roasters (415 641-1024;
   www.ritualroasters.com)
Red Rock Roasters (650 967-4473;
   www.redrockcoffee.org)

**corn & black bean salsa**
Trader Joe's
   (www.traderjoes.com)

**couches & chairs**
IKEA (www.ikea.com)

**fabric**
Britex (415 392-2910;
   www.britexfabric.com)
Discount Fabrics (415 564-7333;
   www.discountfabrics-sf.com)

**foam**
Bob's Foam Factory (510 657-2420;
   www.bobsfoam.com)
Foamorder (415 503-1188;
   www.foamorder.com)
Foam 'n More
   (www.foamforyou.com)

**foamboard**
Arch Supplies (415 433-2724;
   www.archsupplies.com)
ULINE Shipping Supply Specialists
   (800 958-5463; www.uline.com)

**furniture & consulting**
Steelcase (800 333-9939;
   www.steelcase.com)
Oneworkplace (866 632-7010;
   www.oneworkplace.com)

**gas struts & mounting accessories**
McMaster-Carr (630 600-3600;
   www.mcmaster.com)

**hats**
San Gregorio General Store (650 726-0565;
   www.sangregoriostore.com)
Goorin Brothers (415 402-0454;
   www.goorin.com)

Resources_Yours

Jot down your local suppliers

yellow pages

**ice cream**
Mr. and Mrs. Miscellaneous (415 970-0750)
Bi-Rite (415 626-5600;
    www.biritecreamery.com)
Humphry Slocombe (415 550-6971;
    www.humphryslocombe.com)

**magnets**
K&J Magnets (888 746-7556;
    www.kjmagnetics.com)

**manufacturing / fabricating**
HCSI Manufacturing (408 778-8231;
    www.hcsimfg.com)
Because We Can (510 922-8846;
    www.becausewecan.org)
Zomadic, LLC
    (www.zomadic.com)
Monkey Wrench Designs
    (www.mwdes.com)

**moving trucks**
Budget Truck
    (www.budgettruck.com)

**off-site storage**
PODS (877 770-7637; www.pods.com)

**on-line design inspiration**
    www.notcot.org
    www.core77.com
    www.archdaily.com

make space

    www.pinterest.com
    www.flickr.com

**paper**
Kelly Paper (415 522-0420;
    www.kellypaper.com)

**photo fabric banners**
CanvasPop (866 619-9574;
    www.canvaspop.com)

**plastics**
Port Plastics (408 571-2231;
    www.portplastics.com)
TAP Plastics (800 246-5055;
    www.tapplastics.com)

**projection screen material**
Da-Lite (www.da-lite.com)

**prototyping materials & toys**
Thinkgeek (703 293-6299;
    www.thinkgeek.com)
Oriental Trading Company (800 875-8480;
    www.orientaltrading.com)

**sheet metal**
McNichols (www.mcnichols.com)

**showerboard panels**
Pine Cone Lumber (408 736-5491;
    www.pineconelumber.com)

**silk-screening materials**
Pearl Fine Art Supplies (800 451-7327;
    www.pearlpaint.com)

**speedrail pipe & couplers**
Hollaender Mfg. (800 772-8800;
    www.hollaender.com)

**steel rails and trolleys**
Unistrut (www.unistrut.com)
Lord & Sons (800 468-3791;
    www.lordandsons.com)

**swimming goggles**
Palo Alto Toys (650 328-8555;
    www.toyandsport.com)

**tools**
McMaster-Carr (630 600-3600;
    www.mcmaster.com)

**vinyl (bulk materials)**
Product Sign Supplies (800 540-9199;
    www.productsignsupplies.com)

**vinyl cutter**
Roland DGA (www.rolanddga.com)

**workbench legs**
McMaster-Carr (630 600-3600;
    www.mcmaster.com)

Resources_Yours

# Build a space on the cheap.

**Think big in the midst of limited resources and use small changes to make a big difference.**

# Set up a personal studio space.

**Make a space for yourself at home or work.**

# Jump-start an existing space.

**Change your space, how you look at it, and what you do with it. Understand what makes your community unique and alter your space to amplify those strengths.**

## Find other ways to find stuff.

**Check out the other ways to navigate this book and places to get some of the items mentioned within it.**

## Make a space for new ideas.

**Pursue active postures, widely visible work surfaces, and bold customs to encourage a generative culture.**

## Make a space to stay focused.

**Provide space to dig deep and concentrate alone or with others.**

# Make a flexible space.

**Create a space that adapts to the needs of the people who use it and build constraints to inspire new variations.**

# Build a workshop.

**Create a canvas to fill with ideas: a space for spreading out, where materials and tools sit at arm's reach.**

# Shape behavior with space.

**Transform your environment to transform the habits of the people who work there.**

## Create a shared team-space.

**Get people together, keep them moving, and help visualize their ideas & realize collective potential.**

# b-side instructions

**Welcome to the B-Side of make space. You've stumbled on an alternative way to navigate this book. Paul is not dead.***

**make space** is a tool to help you conceive and build new environments for creative work. The tips and recipes within are valid whether your creative work occurs at "work," at school, or at home.

Designing an environment can be a colossal task. It is big in scale, in emotional complexity, and in sheer number of decisions. The content in this book is divided into bits small enough for absorption and action. Those bits are presented as a sequenced shuffle of Tools, Situations, Space Studies, and Insights paired with a Design Template to inspire & support your ideas & actions.

**Perhaps you are already inspired. And... you are ready for action.** We know that one action leads to the next and often it all begins with a seemingly simple question: "How can I... ?" Navigation on the B-Side begins with action. Look over there for guiding actions (in white, at the beginning of each section). Then look to the content suggestions beneath each heading to help you make it happen.

**This is a reference to a band called "The Beatles" that used to produce something called "records" that were believed to contain hidden messages such as "Paul is Dead" when played backwards (Ask your parents).**

*Rock in peace, John and George.

# make space